Friedrich Nietzsche

Titles in the series Critical Lives present the work of leading cultural figures of the modern period. Each book explores the life of the artist, writer, philosopher or architect in question and relates it to their major works.

In the same series

Friedrich Nietzsche

Ritchie Robertson

REAKTION BOOKS

To the many students who over the years have taken my course
'Nietzsche and His Impact'

Published by
REAKTION BOOKS LTD
Unit 32, Waterside
44–48 Wharf Road
London N1 7UX, UK
www.reaktionbooks.co.uk

First published 2022
Copyright © Ritchie Robertson 2022

Printed and bound in Great Britain by TJ Books Ltd, Padstow, Cornwall

A catalogue record for this book is available from the British Library

ISBN 978 1 78914 606 6

Contents

Author's Note

In writing the biographical parts of this book I have drawn heavily on the magisterial three-volume biography by Curt Paul Janz (1978), and am also indebted to the relatively short biography by Ronald Hayman (1980). Two reference books have been invaluable: the *Nietzsche-Handbuch* edited by Henning Ottmann (2000), and the *Companion to Friedrich Nietzsche* edited by Paul Bishop (2012) – the latter, in particular, a treasure-house of solid information accessibly presented. Among recent studies of Nietzsche I have benefited particularly from Robert C. Holub's *Nietzsche in the Nineteenth Century* (2018), one of the few studies to make thorough use of Nietzsche's library.

For Nietzsche's texts and *Nachlass* I have used the fifteen-volume *Kritische Studienausgabe* (*KSA*), itself based on the monumental *Werke* (1968–) edited by Giorgio Colli and Mazzino Montinari. His letters are quoted from the eight-volume *Sämtliche Briefe: Kritische Studienausgabe* (*KSB*), likewise edited by Colli and Montinari. References to Nietzsche's texts are given in parentheses, for example (*GM* III 27) refers to *The Genealogy of Morals*, Book III, section 27; (*BGE* 13) to *Beyond Good and Evil*, section 13.

Ecce Homo is difficult to cite as it is divided into mini-chapters with such titles as 'Why I am So Wise', or the titles of his previous works which he discusses. Hence I have used such abbreviations as (*EH* 'Wise' 1) and (*EH* 'z' 2), where *z* refers to *Thus Spoke Zarathustra*.

Zarathustra itself is cited by book and section number (for example *z* II 1). Although in most editions, confusingly, the sections are not numbered, numbers are provided in Graham Parkes's translation, which in other respects, too, since it contains a good introduction, notes and an index, is an invaluable study aid.

I have quoted from the following translations:

Beyond Good and Evil, trans. R. J. Hollingdale
(Harmondsworth, 1972)
The Birth of Tragedy, trans. Douglas Smith (Oxford, 2000)
On the Genealogy of Morals, trans. Douglas Smith (Oxford, 1996)
Thus Spoke Zarathustra, trans. Graham Parkes (Oxford, 2005)
Twilight of the Idols and *The Anti-Christ*, trans.
R. J. Hollingdale (Harmondsworth, 1968)
Untimely Meditations, trans. R. J. Hollingdale (Cambridge, 1997)

Where no translator is specified, the translation is my own. The same applies to translations from other German and French writers. Quotations from the *Nachlass*, and from texts of which there is no handy translation, are cited as *KSA* with volume and page number.

Abbreviations

The following abbreviations refer to Nietzsche's texts:

A	*The Antichrist*
BGE	*Beyond Good and Evil*
BT	*The Birth of Tragedy*
CW	*The Case of Wagner*
D	*Daybreak*
EH	*Ecce Homo*
GM	*The Genealogy of Morals*
GS	*The Gay Science*
HA	*Human, All-Too-Human*
KSA	*Kritische Studienausgabe*
	(Critical Edition of Nietzsche's Works)
TI	*Twilight of the Idols*
UM	*Untimely Meditations*
VMS	*Vermischte Meinungen und Sprüche*
	(Assorted Opinions and Sayings) in *HA*, Part II
WS	*The Wanderer and His Shadow* in *HA*, Part II
Z	*Thus Spoke Zarathustra*
ZB	*On the Future of our Educational Institutions* in *KSA* I

Nietzsche as a student in Leipzig, *c.* 1868–9.

Introduction

In 1902 W. B. Yeats reported his discovery of Nietzsche, 'that strong enchanter', whose writings gave him a 'curious astringent joy'.[1] From the 1890s onwards, many other readers immersed themselves in Nietzsche's work, often with at least the hint of ambivalence that Yeats conveys here. Among the giants of modernist literature, not only Yeats but D. H. Lawrence, Thomas Mann, Robert Musil, André Gide and many others engaged with Nietzsche, sometimes with blind discipleship but more often with a combination of enthusiasm and critical reserve.[2] Beyond the literary world, Nietzsche appealed to ordinary readers in a way few philosophers have done. It can fairly be claimed that his ideas helped decisively to shape the intellectual outlook of modernity. They also fed into the mental world of fascism, and although it would be unjust to call Nietzsche a herald of the Third Reich and the Holocaust, many passages in his writings – not separable from the rest of his thought, but integral to it – encourage an inhumanity barely imaginable when he was writing. In this book I have tried to be fair to Nietzsche, while avoiding the temptation to sanitize his writings by downplaying the shocking and reprehensible parts.

There were and are excellent reasons for Nietzsche's popularity. He is simply a brilliant writer. His texts – especially those from *Human, All-Too-Human* (1878) onwards, written as series of extended aphorisms – are intensely concentrated and also fast-moving: the argument develops, shifts, turns back on itself, in a way that demands not only close attention but frequent re-reading. The excitement and importance of Nietzsche's enquiries are underlined by the hyperbole and other rhetorical devices that enhance his style.[3] Above all, Nietzsche involves the reader with rhetorical questions and by the use of 'we'. He constantly encourages the reader to become one of the 'free spirits' whom his style seeks to bring into being.

There are negative features to Nietzsche's style. Particularly in the later texts, beginning with *Beyond Good and Evil* (1886) and notably in the jottings assembled as *Twilight of the Idols* (1889), he becomes not just polemical but aggressive, strident, even scurrilous. The subtitle of *Twilight* runs, ominously, 'How to Philosophize with a Hammer'. Some passages may arouse the guilty pleasure one can gain nowadays from reading right-wing newspaper columnists. Although commentators often concentrate on these later writings, calling them the work of the 'mature' Nietzsche, there is good reason to look more closely at his 'middle period' texts (*Human, All-Too-Human*; *Daybreak* (1881); and sections 1–4 of *The Gay Science* (1882)): their radical analyses of psychology and morality, especially when they discuss religion, are often subtler and certainly more measured than the later texts. Then of course there is the extraordinary prose-poem *Thus Spoke Zarathustra* (1883–4), sometimes called his 'philosophical masterpiece'.[4] Even if not that, it is certainly a monumental work of some kind.

Nothing so complimentary can be said about *The Will to Power*, a book whose continued currency is something of a scandal. Nietzsche did not approve its publication. After his collapse, it was compiled by his sister, with the help of various editors, from his voluminous manuscript notes (his *Nachlass*). As Nietzsche had announced in print that he was writing a magnum opus with this title (*GM* III 27), the editors assumed that his notes from the later 1880s were a draft of this work, and arranged the notes systematically under four headings. More recent and more careful scholarship has shown that although Nietzsche did plan a magnum opus, and considered various possible titles and lists of contents, he had abandoned the plan by 3 September 1888.[5] Since the notes were made for Nietzsche's own use, and were never polished for publication, the literary merit of *The Will to Power* is far below that of Nietzsche's published works. It is not a fabrication – Nietzsche did write its contents – but it comes across as an angry monologue, rather than the dialogue which Nietzsche conducts with the reader in his published texts.

Should one nevertheless draw on *The Will to Power* when trying to expound Nietzsche's thought? Although some major studies of Nietzsche do so,[6] there are several reasons not to. As the *Nachlass* has now been expertly edited by Giorgio Colli and Mazzino Montinari, one should go straight there. The *Nachlass* is fascinating, especially for its information about Nietzsche's reading, and sometimes helps to clarify obscurities in the published works. But if Nietzsche's manuscript notes correspond to the content of his published texts, one doesn't need them; and if they differ from the published texts, they may express ideas that Nietzsche was simply trying out, that he rejected or that for whatever reason he did not wish to publish.

Moreover, *The Will to Power* misrepresents Nietzsche by making him seem too systematic. Nietzsche's only full-length and systematic treatises are *The Birth of Tragedy*, *The Genealogy of Morals* and *The Antichrist*, and even they are full of digressions. Nietzsche thought continually and intensely. Many of his thoughts came to him when he was out walking, or when he was prostrated by illness. He jotted them down as best he could, and in spells of remission he worked them into aphorisms, rarely of more than about three pages, sometimes arranged in loose thematic clusters. His thought therefore consists of a galaxy of brilliant ideas which he was not in a position to harmonize (he often wrote without copies of his earlier books to hand). While his thought has a broad coherence and continuity, therefore, it also shows major apparent (and not so apparent) contradictions. Life is will to power (*BGE* 13), but there is no such thing as the will (*D* 124). Life should consist in self-overcoming (*Z* II 12), but the self is an illusion (*BGE* 54). 'Nothing is true' (*GM* III 24), but one should serve truth (*A* 50) and reject lies (especially lies told by priests, *A* 58).

There is limited value in trying to iron out Nietzsche's many contradictions. The broad lines of his thought are clear enough. It would be futile to try to reconstruct a single, univocal philosophy that exists somewhere behind Nietzsche's texts. In doing so, one would be ignoring Nietzsche's repeated warnings against searching for a metaphysical 'true world' hidden behind phenomena (see *TI*: 'How the "true world" became a fable'). With Nietzsche, what you read is what you get. Moreover, Nietzsche often presents his ideas explicitly as hypotheses or speculations, in aphorisms beginning 'Suppose that . . .' or 'Assuming that . . .'. He is not so much proclaiming a doctrine as encouraging his readers to think independently.

Above all, since Nietzsche's style is inimitable, one is at least doing him a disservice, and perhaps making him harder to understand, by translating his thoughts entirely into the sober, grey language of academic philosophy. Analytic philosophers have seldom acknowledged this problem, perhaps because, at least in teaching, they rely so much on translations.[7] Of course one should not try to imitate Nietzsche's style, but when a serious interpreter tells us 'Nietzsche proceeds to observe that, taken together, normative objectivism and the rejection of descriptive objectivism entail nihilism,' something has gone wrong.[8] Text and interpretation have moved too far apart.

Since Nietzsche's texts present such an overwhelming wealth of ideas, it is hardly surprising that his expositors have differed so widely. Martin Heidegger went so far as to claim that Nietzsche's published texts were merely the 'foreground' to his thought, which was really contained in *The Will to Power*. After the Second World War, Walter Kaufmann took the lead in trying to free Nietzsche from the associations of Nazism.[9] Kaufmann's presentation of Nietzsche as centrally concerned with culture and the individual is attractive and largely persuasive, but still one-sided. Another way to sanitize Nietzsche was to take him out of history and interpret him as concerned with language, fiction and the impossibility of truth: this 'new Nietzsche' was largely a French creation.[10] In the English-speaking world, philosophers trained in the analytic tradition started to take an interest in Nietzsche and assess his works by standards of careful philosophical argument.[11]

It was still necessary, however, to put Nietzsche back into history.[12] Recent research has investigated Nietzsche's reading, using the notes and references in his *Nachlass* and his personal library, which, being kept in the Nietzsche Archive at Weimar, was normally inaccessible to Western scholars until after the demise of the German Democratic Republic. Nietzsche read intensively and annotated his books in detail.[13] Often these were books on the natural sciences. Although his post-war commentators sought to reclaim Nietzsche for cultural and even humanist values, it must now be admitted that he did not acknowledge any opposition between humanist and physical science, both being *Wissenschaft*, and read extensively in biology, physiology, physics and thermodynamics.[14] He was convinced that philosophy, to say anything valuable about the world, must be abreast of the latest scientific knowledge, although he also often disputed the claims made by scientists.

In this introductory study I have tried not only to place Nietzsche's writings in a biographical framework, in keeping with the aims of the Critical Lives series, but to suggest something of his nineteenth-century context. I have at all times referred closely to Nietzsche's actual words, principally of course in his published texts but also in his letters and, where appropriate, in the *Nachlass*.

The recollections of contemporaries collected by Sander L. Gilman in *Conversations with Nietzsche* (1991) have also been valuable.

My own approach to Nietzsche is to take him at his word when he claims to be continuing the Enlightenment. Although Nietzsche says many incompatible and sometimes illogical things about truth, a strong thread running through his writings is the search for truth. He admits many times that truth about the world is difficult to obtain, that it is often unpleasant, that it may often be better for people not to know the truth and content themselves with stimulating fictions. But he himself repeatedly formulates the ideal of *Redlichkeit* (honesty, integrity) as guiding his enquiries. The service of truth may require one to abandon cherished illusions: 'the service of truth is the hardest service. – What does it mean to be *upright* in intellectual matters? That one is severe on one's heart, that one despises "fine feelings", that one makes every Yea and Nay into an issue of conscience!' (*A* 50). In this respect, Nietzsche is an heir to Immanuel Kant, who in his famous essay 'An Answer to the Question: What Is Enlightenment?' said that the watchword of enlightenment is 'Have the courage to use your *own* intellect!'[15] Reading Nietzsche is a constant summons to think for oneself, to argue back and often to disagree profoundly with Nietzsche – but also to be honest with oneself about why one disagrees.

1
The Philologist

The author of devastating attacks on Christianity was, appropriately, the son of a clergyman. Friedrich Wilhelm Nietzsche was born on 15 October 1844 and named after the king of Prussia, with whom he shared a birthday. His father, Karl Ludwig Nietzsche, was the Lutheran pastor in the village of Röcken in Saxony in central Germany. Ludwig Nietzsche and his wife Franziska, née Oehler, had two more children, Elisabeth (1846–1935) and Joseph, who died early in 1849, just before his second birthday. Born in 1813, Ludwig was a tall, good-looking man whose time spent officiating at a ducal court had left him with a dignified bearing and a conservative outlook. Franziska (1826–1897) was devout, imperfectly educated, practical and sensible, trained to be a devoted wife and mother. They shared the parsonage with Ludwig's mother Erdmuthe, who dominated the household and controlled its finances, and his ailing and neurotic sisters Rosalie and Auguste.

Family life was upset when Ludwig Nietzsche fell ill in September 1848. Dizzy spells, periodical aphasia, migraines and eventual blindness led up to his death on 30 July 1849. It is impossible to be sure what his illness was. The doctors spoke vaguely of 'softening of the brain'. Modern suggestions include a cerebral haemorrhage, a brain tumour or cerebral tuberculosis. Something may have been contributed by Ludwig's distress at the 1848 revolutions. In March, on learning that the king of Prussia had negotiated with the Berlin insurrectionists and even appeared in public with the

Nietzsche's parents, Pastor Karl Ludwig Nietzsche and Franziska Nietzsche, née Oehler.

cockade symbolizing liberty on his hat, Ludwig had burst into tears, and afterwards he forbade his family ever to speak of these events. Whatever the causes, the little boy, known as 'Fritz', was obliged to witness the slow collapse of his affectionate father.

Required to vacate the parsonage, the family moved to the nearby town of Naumburg, which had some 15,000 inhabitants. Naumburg retained its medieval quarter, its cathedral and its town walls, with a gate that was locked every night at 10 p.m. Here they moved into a small house, of which Erdmuthe and her daughters occupied the front portion and Franziska and her children the darker, more cramped rear part. Fritz was initially sent to the local primary school, so that he should mix with boys from other social classes, but this was not a success: the others regarded him, with his prim manners, as an oddity, and mocked him as 'the little pastor'. After a year Fritz and two other middle-class boys, Gustav Krug and Wilhelm Pinder, were sent to a private school which prepared them to enter the Dom-Gymnasium (Cathedral Grammar School) in 1854. The three boys remained close friends for many years.

So Nietzsche's was hardly a happy childhood. He idolized the memory of his father. In 1884 he told a friend about 'my father's *extraordinary* nature; all who knew him considered him an angel rather than human' (to Overbeck, 14 September 1884). In his eccentric autobiography *Ecce Homo*, written in 1888, he says what a privilege it was to have had such a father, whom the farmers he preached to compared to an angel (*EH* 'Wise' 3). Bereaved, he could not fall back on his mother's love. Franziska Nietzsche clearly had many sterling qualities, was devoted to her two surviving children, made them eat a healthy diet with ample fruit and vegetables, and encouraged activities such as swimming and skating. But she could not enter into her gifted son's mental world. Worse, she gave an impression of emotional coldness. Children need not only to be loved, but to feel loved. Her son always felt remote from her and often hostile to her. In *Ecce Homo*, admittedly a wildly unbalanced book, he writes: 'When I seek the deepest antithesis to myself, the

The 13th-century cathedral at Naumburg, the town where Nietzsche grew up, photographed *c.* 1897.

incalculable vulgarity of instincts, I always find my mother and sister' (*EH* 'Wise' 4). Only weeks after writing this, Nietzsche would collapse into insanity and be tended selflessly by his mother until her death in 1897.

An anecdote from Nietzsche's primary-school days, related by his sister, is revealing. One afternoon, as school was ending, there came a torrential downpour. All the other boys rushed home, but young Fritz walked home sedately, and, when rebuked by his mother for getting drenched, explained that the school rules forbade running and jumping. Evidently his detachment from the others overrode the imitative instinct which governs much social behaviour. That and his rigid obedience to rules suggest that he belonged somewhere on the autistic spectrum. Such detachment can be the precondition for eccentricity, originality or both. In addition, not only had Fritz thoroughly internalized the school rules, but their authority rested for him on the authority of his dead father, who was beyond criticism or resistance, and whose dignified manner he was trying to reproduce. The child's condescending explanation of his conduct sounds as though he were assuming his father's role of superiority to his mother; although it seems priggish, it might charitably be interpreted as a search for approval from the internalized image of his father. In enduring the discomfort of getting soaked, he was also manifesting the will that would sustain him in adult life and form the central theme of his philosophy. Later in life, while continuing to identify with his idealized father, Nietzsche would also rebel against him in his vehement opposition to Christianity.

Although warmth and fun were in short supply in Nietzsche's childhood, they were not absent. He was close to his sister, who hero-worshipped him. They made up stories, some focusing on a small china squirrel whom they called King Squirrel I. He wrote poems and developed a love of music after being enraptured, at the age of nine, by the Hallelujah Chorus from Handel's *Messiah* performed in the town church. His mother, although not well off, bought him a piano, and within two years he was able to play sonatas by Beethoven. The parents of his friends Krug and Pinder encouraged him to explore music and literature: when he was twelve, Pinder Senior first introduced him to Goethe. Nietzsche made no additional friends at school: Wilhelm Pinder later recalled him as solitary, melancholy and hard-working, but also as taking the lead in their games and ingenious in making their games more challenging.

The next stage of Nietzsche's education began in October 1858, when his outstanding school record gained him a free place at the famous boarding school Pforta, a few kilometres from Naumburg. This was an extraordinary institution. Its alumni included the poet Friedrich Gottlob Klopstock (1724–1803), well known for his Protestant epic *The Messiah*; the philosopher Johann Gottlieb Fichte (1762–1814); and the great historian Leopold von Ranke (1795–1886). Originally a Cistercian monastery, but transformed into a school at the Reformation, its extensive grounds were still enclosed by a wall, and it retained its own chapel. Although it might resemble

Cloisters at Pforta, Nietzsche's boarding school.

an English public school, it was distinguished by its specific educational mission of fostering high-grade students of the classics, many of whom, it was expected, would proceed to academic careers. It was also a 'total institution' that aimed to mould the boys' characters.[1] This was done through a strict timetable. The boys had to be out of bed by 5 a.m. in summer, 6 a.m. in winter. Lessons and supervised preparation occupied most of the day. Boys were allowed outside the school grounds only between 4 and 6 p.m. on Sundays. There was plenty of recreation: swimming, games, gymnastics and occasional outings in the form of military-style marches and patriotic demonstrations, affirming loyalty to the king of Prussia. Nietzsche sang in the school choir and took part in the plays that the students put on at Shrovetide.

The curriculum was dominated by the study of classical languages. The boys had six hours of Greek every week and eleven of Latin in the first three years, ten in the last three. German (in which Nietzsche stood out through his excellent essays) and mathematics (which bored him) were also important. History and religious knowledge (including Hebrew) were taught; natural science, apart from physics, was absent. The boys acquired thorough familiarity with the Greek and Latin classics. In November 1861 the seventeen-year-old Nietzsche tells his sister that in Greek he is reading Homer, the orator Lysias and Herodotus, and in Latin Virgil, Livy, Cicero and Sallust. The boys probably left Pforta with a better knowledge of the classics than many present-day university graduates. Modern languages were available only as optional extras offered by enthusiastic teachers. Nietzsche reports joining reading groups in French and Italian, but he did not become very proficient in either language. His later French reading required him often to consult a dictionary. He seems never to have learned much English, but read Shakespeare, Byron and Shelley in translation.

Nietzsche was still an outstanding pupil, usually top of the class in his first three years; latterly he relaxed his efforts somewhat.

Nietzsche at Pforta, 1861, photograph by Louis Held.

Occasionally did he kick over the traces, but even then only mildly. In November 1862, having to report on the condition of classroom furniture, he wrote in a humorous tone, whereupon he was summoned before the authorities and sentenced to three hours' detention with temporary loss of Sunday privileges. The following April, on a Sunday outing, he and a fellow student drank too much beer and unfortunately encountered a teacher; Nietzsche was degraded from first to third place in his class and lost an hour of his Sunday free time. This seems a heavy-handed way to treat an eighteen-year-old. The contrition with which Nietzsche reports the latter incident to his mother also sounds excessive, as though he had thoroughly internalized the school's discipline.

His sister reports a more unusual incident. Some boys were talking about Mucius Scaevola, the Roman hero who, as Livy recounts, demonstrated his courage by thrusting his right hand into a fire. When a boy expressed horror at this act, Nietzsche placed some lighted matches in the palm of his own hand and endured the pain, receiving serious burns, until someone knocked the matches away. This seemingly pointless gesture has been interpreted as sado-masochism;[2] at any rate, it suggests a desire to advertise the strength of his own will.

Nietzsche's studies at Pforta were sometimes hampered by the ill health that would torment him for much of his life. At the age of twelve he had been diagnosed as short-sighted. He wore glasses for reading, and dark glasses to keep off strong sunlight. Later in life he would have spells of near blindness. It must be remembered that before electric light, people were dependent on natural light, however dim, and on lamps and candles, all of which put a strain on weak eyesight. The school's medical records reveal that Nietzsche was often in the sick-bay with influenza, rheumatism and headaches. These must have been bad, since the school aimed to make its students physically tough and would not have sent him to the sick-bay for minor ailments.

Nevertheless, and despite the rigorous regime of study (for which he was afterwards grateful), Nietzsche cultivated private interests and developed his independence of mind, sometimes more than the teachers liked. In 1861, aged seventeen, he decided that his favourite poet was Friedrich Hölderlin (1770–1843), who had succumbed to insanity in about 1806 and was then little known, although now regarded as the greatest German poet after Goethe. Hölderlin was also a classicist, and his work is steeped in the literature and culture of ancient Greece. Submitting a German essay on Hölderlin, Nietzsche, thinking of the famous diatribe against the Germans in the novel *Hyperion* (1797), praised him also for attacking German philistinism. The teacher who corrected his essay advised him to find a 'healthier, clearer, more German poet', thereby unwittingly confirming Hölderlin's judgement. Nietzsche's second favourite around this time was a *less* German poet, namely Byron: not, however, the Byron of *Don Juan*, but the author of such plays as the Faustian *Manfred* and the Venetian tragedy *The Two Foscari*. Although little read now, Byron's plays were important to his Europe-wide reputation: they were, for example, much admired by Goethe, who unlike Nietzsche could read them in English.

Other interests point forward. Like many imaginative young people, Nietzsche was fascinated by the world of Germanic legend.[3] For about four years his interest focused on the Gothic king Ermanaric, who appears in the Eddas and some sagas. Nietzsche read about him there and in works by medieval Latin historians, and planned a symphonic poem about him. He was also much taken by the grandiose Old Norse concept of Ragnarök, the end of the world. This early interest no doubt helped him later to appreciate Richard Wagner's use of Germanic mythology, especially in the *Ring* cycle ending with *Götterdämmerung*.

A particularly ambitious essay commenting on the first chorus in Sophocles' *Oedipus Rex* led Nietzsche to reflect on the origins of tragedy. He traced it back to lyric poetry and described it as essentially musical, contrasting it with modern opera, in which the libretto assumed undue importance by being merely set to music by the composer. The great exception to this modern tendency was Wagner. Although Nietzsche in 1864 was not yet a fully fledged Wagnerian, this distinction is the germ of the case made for Wagner's music-dramas in *The Birth of Tragedy* (1872).

Another momentous encounter was with the writings of the American thinker Ralph Waldo Emerson (1803–1882), which Nietzsche first read (in German translation) in 1862 and to which he constantly returned. His surviving copies of Emerson's books are full of enthusiastic marginalia. He transcribed many sentences from Emerson into his notebooks, where he also wrote, under the heading 'Emerson': 'I have never felt so much at home, in my own home, in a book – it is so close to me that I cannot praise it' (KSA IX 588). In 1883 he said he felt Emerson was a 'brother-soul' (to Overbeck, 24 December). Yet it is difficult to assess just what Nietzsche owed to him. Although it has been claimed that Nietzsche owed most of his central ideas to Emerson, it is hard to distinguish Emerson's influence from that of others.[4]

Emerson's presence is clearest in Nietzsche's essay 'Schopenhauer as Educator' (1874), which quotes Emerson twice. At the outset Nietzsche deplores the readiness of most people to deny their own individuality and conform to the herd: this is the theme of Emerson's essay 'Self-Reliance', which urges that one should dare to trust oneself and ignore majority opinion. 'To believe your own thought, to believe that what is true for you in your own private heart is true for all men, – that is genius.' Since society demands conformity, 'to be great is to be misunderstood.'[5] Urging readers to have the courage to go their own way, Nietzsche adds: 'Who was it who uttered the sentence: "A man never rises higher than when he does not know whither his way will lead him"?' The answer is Cromwell, whom Nietzsche found quoted in Emerson's essay 'Circles'.[6] Near the end of 'Schopenhauer as Educator' Nietzsche quotes Emerson's claim that a great thinker is dangerous because his thought can revolutionize the entire system of things. We can at least say, therefore, that Emerson encouraged Nietzsche to cultivate individuality, to despise the herd, to pursue truth at all costs and to accept isolation. It may even be from Emerson that Nietzsche first learned about the sage Zarathustra, who is quoted in 'Self-Reliance'.

Nietzsche made few friends at Pforta. He gradually got to know Paul Deussen, another pastor's son, who in later life became a distinguished scholar of Indian religion, and then an aristocrat and devoted musician, Carl von Gersdorff, to whom Nietzsche, especially in the later 1860s, would confide many intimate reflections in letters. He kept in touch with his Naumburg friends Pinder and Krug, meeting them in the school holidays. At Nietzsche's instigation, in 1860 they formed a society solemnly called 'Germania', each member undertaking to produce every month a poem, an essay, a musical composition or an architectural design and submit it to the others for criticism. This society was important for Nietzsche, not least because Krug was an early enthusiast of Wagner. Nietzsche, whose favourite composer was Schumann, was more reserved, but his sister recalls how he and Krug used to hold 'Wagner orgies' by repeatedly playing a setting of *Tristan und Isolde* on the piano. 'Germania' broke up in 1863, partly because Nietzsche was too merciless in criticizing his friends' productions. This habit of assuming critical authority with little regard for others' feelings, acquired by domineering over his adoring sister, would reappear later in Nietzsche's relations with others, and also lies behind the relentlessly aggressive tone of many of his later writings.

Nietzsche's independence of mind appears also in his changing attitude to religion. It was taken for granted that he would follow his father into the Church. Occasionally he did show a piety that would have pleased his mother. Deussen tells us that when he and Nietzsche were confirmed on 10 March 1861, they had an exalted feeling of devotion. If so, it did not last. Later that year Nietzsche advised his sister to read a recent life of Jesus written in a rationalist spirit, and asked for Ludwig Feuerbach's *The Essence of Christianity* (1841) as a birthday present. Feuerbach maintains that religion consists in feeling, not reason: the substantive content of religion is merely the projection of human values onto an imaginary God; as humanity acquires self-knowledge, and philosophy develops at the expense of religion, we become aware of our values and find ways of realizing them in actual life. The other great anti-Christian work of the day (though not so intended by its author) was *The Life of Jesus Critically Examined* (1835–6) by David Strauss, which explained the alleged supernatural events in the Gospels as myths of the kind that naturally grow up around an exceptional individual. At Easter in 1865 Nietzsche refused to take Communion, much to his mother's distress; they quarrelled, but agreed to avoid the subject of religion, which, in view of his mother's strong piety and Nietzsche's deepening aversion, placed further strain on their relations.

At least Nietzsche could explain his standpoint to his sister with some hope of being understood. In a letter of 11 June 1865, he pointed out that the difficulty of a belief was no guarantee of its truth, as she supposed. 'It is difficult to believe that 2×2 is not 4; is it therefore truer?' Faith had its own value, but it was irrelevant to the objective truth of a belief. The enquirer after truth could not be satisfied with faith. 'For the true enquirer, the result of his enquiry surely doesn't matter. In our enquiries, are we seeking calm, peace, happiness? No, only truth, even if it were repellent and hideous.' Certain further thoughts, antithetical to Christian ethics, Nietzsche confided only to a private notebook. One should treat other people kindly, but remember that they only existed in order to serve one's own ends. Every action that is necessary is thereby justified. 'If an immoral action is necessary, then it is moral for us.'[7]

Such views seem strange coming from someone destined for the Church, but by the time he formulated them, Nietzsche had already abandoned the study of theology. He arrived at the University of Bonn in October 1864, having chosen that university mainly because Deussen was going there too. Although he registered as a student of theology, he attended more lectures on such subjects as classical literature, politics and art history, and in general pursued his studies in a dilettante way. In his second semester he changed his main subject to philology, thus inflicting another disappointment on his mother. He also attended the theatre and musical events, including a concert given by the pianist Clara Schumann, and himself sang in the Bonn city choir.

Too much of Nietzsche's time, however, was spent trying to integrate himself into student culture by joining a fraternity (*Burschenschaft*). These fraternities, founded as patriotic societies for military training in the war against Napoleon, with names such as Franconia (the one Nietzsche joined), Thuringia or Rhenania, had largely abandoned their original democratic principles. Their main activities, governed by a rulebook called the *Comment*, were ritualized beer-drinking (at sessions called *Kneipe* or *Commers*) and duelling (*Mensur*). The point of duelling was not to injure your opponent but to receive a mild wound which would be stitched up carelessly, leaving a scar as proof of your manhood. Nietzsche himself fought an entirely good-natured duel with a fellow student and had the satisfaction of receiving a cut above the bridge of his nose. The in-group language of the fraternities extended further: a new member, such as Nietzsche, was a *Fuchs* (fox); anyone who did not belong to a fraternity was a *Kamel* (camel, presumably because they were out in the desert). After graduating, you remained a member of your fraternity (one of the 'elder gentlemen', or *Alte Herren*) and were encouraged to revisit it and to support other members, so that the fraternities were a highly durable old-boy network.

Despite his efforts, Nietzsche could not take to the beer-swilling, or to the arrogant naivety with which his fellows voiced their political opinions. On leaving Bonn he did not formally resign from Franconia, but sent a letter of resignation later, telling them they needed to grow up; this advice went down very badly, and the Franconians expelled him permanently. His experience of fraternities helps to account for the denunciations of the German character which pepper Nietzsche's later writings, and especially for the polemic against student beer-drinking in *Twilight of the Idols* ('What the Germans lack', 2).

Nietzsche's time in Bonn also included an incident which needs to be related, if only because a legend has grown up around it. Our sole source is the memoir that Deussen published after Nietzsche's death. Deussen writes:

> I am slightly reluctant to tell here a story which deserves to be rescued from the past for what it reveals about Nietzsche's way of thinking. One day in February 1865 he had gone by himself to Cologne, had been shown the sights by a guide, and finally asked the latter to take him to a restaurant. The guide, however, led him into a house of ill repute. 'Suddenly,' Nietzsche told me the next day, 'I saw myself surrounded by half a dozen apparitions in gauze and tinsel who were looking at me expectantly. I stood for a while speechless. Then I went over instinctively to a piano, as the only being there with a soul, and struck a few chords. That ended my paralysis and I made my escape.' From this and everything I know about Nietzsche, I am inclined to believe that the words apply to him: *mulierem nunquam tetigit* [he never touched a woman].[8]

Thomas Mann, who drew on Deussen's memoir for many traits of Adrian Leverkühn, the hero of his *Doctor Faustus* (1947), not only used this but made Leverkühn return later, attracted by a particular prostitute, and have sex with her although she warned him that she was syphilitic, imagining that infection would release his creativity.

It was long supposed that the illness which led to Nietzsche's collapse into insanity at the age of 44 resulted from syphilitic infection. The doctors who examined him after his breakdown in January 1889 thought he was suffering from tertiary syphilis. Recently, however, it has been argued that his symptoms were incompatible with syphilis and entirely compatible with a kind of brain tumour, called a retro-orbital meningioma, which must have been growing for much of his life.[9]

At that time, and for long afterwards, it was common for German students to change universities. Heinrich Heine, for example, studied in the 1820s at the universities of Bonn, Göttingen and Berlin. Nietzsche moved in October 1865 to Leipzig. His reasons were that Bonn was too expensive and that his friend Gersdorff, who had been studying in Göttingen but did not like it, was moving there. Such moves were often motivated by the desire to hear lectures from a famous professor, and it has sometimes been supposed that Nietzsche moved because the eminent classical scholar Friedrich Ritschl was leaving Bonn for a chair at Leipzig, but in fact Nietzsche made his decision before Ritschl's move became generally known.

Nietzsche was now committing himself to the study of philology. This meant the study of the Greek and Latin languages and literature, with close attention to textual scholarship: examining the genesis and transmission of literary texts with a view to establishing the most accurate version possible. Textual scholarship is still an important part of classical studies, although they now take a much broader approach to the ancient world. Nietzsche's work at Leipzig consisted of specialized technical studies such as would nowadays be done by doctoral students. Although his enthusiasm for philology would wane, he always considered it the paradigm of intellectual rigour. It was 'the art of accurate reading' and scrupulous interpretation (*HA* 270), carefully bracketing out ideological prejudices and thus incompatible with Christianity. 'A hallmark of the theologian is his incapacity for philology' (A 52): the exegesis of biblical texts was always corrupted by dishonest attempts to prove a theological case. Philology illustrated the discipline that Nietzsche commended in all scholarship (his word *Wissenschaft* comprehends both the humanities and the natural sciences): for the amateur, he says, 'the rigour of its service, this inexorability in great and small things, this rapidity in evaluating, judging, condemning, has something dizzying and frightening' (GS 293); as in the army, you get no praise for getting things right, only a reprimand if you make a mistake.

Ritschl was Nietzsche's main guide in this discipline. Although they had had little contact at Bonn, Ritschl recognized Nietzsche among the audience at his inaugural lecture and greeted him cordially. Ritschl encouraged his most gifted students, including Nietzsche, to form a Philological Society, where they read papers to one another (Ritschl being absent). At the society's second meeting Nietzsche read a paper on Theognis of Megara, a Greek elegiac poet who flourished in the sixth century BCE and whom he had already worked on at Pforta. Afterwards he showed the paper to Ritschl. Some days later Ritschl summoned Nietzsche to his office, asked him about his previous studies and said that he had never known a student who, in only his third semester, produced work so methodologically rigorous and so carefully argued. He urged Nietzsche to publish his work in book form. In the event it appeared as a substantial article two years later in the *Rheinisches Museum für Philologie*, a journal Ritschl edited. Nietzsche was in turn impressed by Ritschl's friendliness, his informality and his tireless concern for his students, regretting only that Ritschl took no interest in philosophy. Ritschl's help extended further. He knew that Nietzsche was doing some work on Diogenes Laertius, who in the third century CE wrote in Greek a series of portraits of the ancient Greek philosophers. When the annual prize essay in philology was announced, its title, chosen by Ritschl, was 'On the Sources of Diogenes Laertius'. Nietzsche entered the competition,

Carl von Gersdorff, Erwin Rohde and Nietzsche, 1871.

submitted his essay in July 1867 with a motto from Pindar, 'Become who you are,' and was awarded the prize.

Nietzsche's studies kept him busy. They also included an essay on the mythical poetic contest between Homer and Hesiod. Drawing partly on Theognis, Nietzsche took this as an example of the *agon*, the competition, which was a central feature of Greek culture and one source of its achievements. Here Nietzsche showed his originality by unwittingly anticipating the arguments put forward by Jacob Burckhardt, the great Swiss historian who would later become a friend, in his lectures on Greek cultural history.[10] Meanwhile Nietzsche enjoyed an unusually (for him) active social life, mostly with fellow students of philology. They included Erwin Rohde, another member of the Philological Society, who would remain a lifelong friend and become a distinguished classical scholar. Rohde and Nietzsche took riding lessons together, and in August 1867 they made a long walking tour in the Bohemian Forest. It has been noted that Rohde was the only friend to whom Nietzsche did not adopt a superior tone.[11]

Despite discouraging noises from Ritschl, Nietzsche became increasingly attached to philosophy. His choice to study Dionysus Laertius' philosophical biographies looks like an attempt to include some philosophy in his philology. At Leipzig, however, he encountered two modern philosophers who had a profound impact on him: Arthur Schopenhauer (1788–1860) and Friedrich Albert Lange (1828–1875).

In October 1865, in a Leipzig bookshop, Nietzsche bought on impulse a copy of Schopenhauer's great work, *The World as Will and Representation* (1819). Reading it that evening in his lodgings, he became absorbed. He felt, he said later, as though the book had been written specially for him. 'I am one of those readers of Schopenhauer who when they have read one page of him know for certain they will go on to read all the pages and will pay heed to every word he ever said' (*UM* 133).

From its first sentence – 'The world is my representation' – onwards, Schopenhauer's work is an original exposition of radical idealism, written in a masterly style that creates a compelling individual voice. The world consists of will and representation. From the outside, the world is my representation. I do not see the sun; I see my mental representation, which I call the sun. From the inside, the world is the Will. The Will is a single force which drives everything that happens. This is the key to understanding the inner essence of the whole of Nature. The Will manifests itself not only in the desires and appetites that animate all living creatures, but in the growth of plants, in the force that makes the magnet seek the pole, in the laws of attraction governing the chemical elements, and in the force of gravity itself. It manifests itself of course in what we call love, the force that draws a man and woman together in the delusion that they are made for each other, when all that is at stake is the blind urge of the Will to perpetuate the species. The Will is that inaccessible ultimate reality that Kant called the *Ding an sich*, the 'thing in itself', and although we cannot access it, we can get close to it in hearing music, for music is the voice of the Will. This is Schopenhauer's explanation of the well-known aesthetic paradox that great music is clearly telling us something important which cannot be put into words or detached in any way from the musical experience.

Thanks to the blind force of the Will, we are, like King Lear, bound upon a wheel of fire. How can we escape? One escape from the pressure of the Will is offered by love: not sexual love, but the love of which the great religious mystics speak. Schopenhauer was familiar with Christian mystical writers and above all with the religious philosophies of Hinduism and Buddhism. He read their scriptures in German, Latin and English translation (he had been educated partly in London, at a school in Wimbledon, and used to read *The Times* every day). If you are inspired by love, you will first try to relieve the sufferings of others. The supreme value that Schopenhauer sees in our interactions with other people is compassion. Pain is an unmitigated evil, and the relief of pain must be good. He writes with particular indignation about the torture of animals in laboratory experiments. But beyond that, the good person may proceed to renounce the Will altogether, to abandon desire. History tells us of people who conquered vast territories, but they are mere puppets of the Will, far inferior to the saints and mystics who renounce the world by overcoming the will to live. This theme in Schopenhauer lies behind the frequent references to 'redemption' and 'sanctification' that occur in Nietzsche's earlier works.

Non-mystics can at least escape temporarily from the Will through art. When we appreciate a work of art, we do not want anything from it. It gives us, in Kant's famous phrase, disinterested pleasure. The pressure of the Will is momentarily abated. Aesthetic contemplation, even of trivial subjects, as in Dutch still-lifes, is therefore pleasurable. Similarly, Nietzsche later writes: 'The hardest and final task of the artist is the portrayal of what is constant, self-contained, lofty, simple, avoiding individual details' (*VMS* 177); he finds this ideal realized in the seventeenth-century painter Claude Lorrain, and wishes for a poetic counterpart. He would find such a counterpart in Adalbert Stifter's *Der Nachsommer* (Indian Summer, 1857), a novel set in the Austrian countryside and filled with landscape evocations which its admirers find spell-binding and its detractors soporific.[12] The artist of genius, according to Schopenhauer, is someone in whom the Will – that is, the blind appetite that drives us to desire, fulfilment, dissatisfaction and renewed futile desire – is relatively weak, and the power of contemplation relatively strong. Hence the artist is able to create works that are objective because they are not the expression of appetite. This conception of artistic objectivity would become an essential part of Nietzsche's outlook.

Finally, Nietzsche took from Schopenhauer an outlook for which 'elitism' is far too mild a term. Ordinary people, in Schopenhauer's view, are mere 'factory-products of nature, such as she brings forth by thousands every day'.[13] The only people who matter are geniuses, who are necessarily isolated in their own time but form an invisible republic, calling to each other across the ages, over the heads of innumerable pygmies. Nietzsche's thought always rests on the conviction that the most valuable element in history is the existence of geniuses and great men.

Nietzsche remained a devotee of Schopenhauer for about a decade. He shared his devotion with Rohde and other friends. But what he admired in Schopenhauer was not primarily the philosophy. As early as 1868 he found fault with it, noting that since the Will is just as inaccessible as Kant's *Ding an sich*, anything Schopenhauer says about it can only be a poetic fantasy, and if the Will is to be understood as the intellect, it must be in the world and not lurking behind it.[14] He liked Schopenhauer's concepts of artistic objectivity and of the genius as the exceptional and supremely important human being. He also admired Schopenhauer as a stylist, and in his earlier books one can see a debt to Schopenhauer's pungent phrasing and skilfully constructed periodic sentences. Above all, his admiration for Schopenhauer was ethical. Schopenhauer was devoted to truth; he preserved his independence of mind by abandoning academic philosophy and pursuing his own original thoughts; he accepted the solitude that was the fate of the genius. Nietzsche would set this out later in the essay 'Schopenhauer as Educator'.

Strictly as a philosophical mentor, Schopenhauer had less influence on Nietzsche than did F. A. Lange. In 1866 Nietzsche discovered Lange's *History of Materialism* (1865), still acknowledged as a major work in the history of philosophy, which traces the idea of materialism from the Greek pre-Socratic philosophers down to nineteenth-century natural science. Nietzsche would continue reading Lange long after he had cooled towards Schopenhauer; he read also the second, revised edition of Lange's book which appeared in 1887. He recommended the book enthusiastically to his friend Gersdorff, mentioning especially Lange's discussions of Democritus, Darwin and Kant (end of August 1866).

Lange regards materialism as the first explanation of the world that suggested itself to the earliest philosophers. Thus Democritus, in the sixth century BCE, surmised that the world consisted of atoms which gradually cohered to form physical objects; the soul consisted only of finer atoms. Materialism brought forth a counter-philosophy in Plato's idea of an imperishable world of timeless Forms or Ideas, and 'the idea that the phenomenal world is only the distorted copy of another world of real objects runs through the whole history of human thought.'[15] This idea even underlay biology until Darwin, in the conception of fixed species; Darwin showed that distinct species are illusory and that the organic world is always, albeit gradually, in flux. However, both materialism and its antithesis are, in Lange's view, mistaken. Materialism cannot account for consciousness, for intellectual activity or for the relation between external movement and sensation (if I am cut by a knife, why do I feel pain?).

The crucial chapter for Nietzsche was Lange's discussion of Kant. Kant refuted naive materialism by showing that all experience requires some prior knowledge. We can experience only what the organization of our minds allows us to experience. But Kant distinguished between the phenomenal world, perceived by our senses, and a 'noumenal' or intelligible world, the *Ding an sich*, accessible only to the intellect. Lange rejects the *Ding an sich* as 'a supposed hypothetical object that lies beyond any possible experience'.[16] It is simply a figment of our imagination. We may like to imagine that something exists which is antithetical to our experience, but such a notion is merely Platonism in a new guise. It is a poetic fiction – which does not mean that it is absurd. 'Kant would not understand, what Plato before him would not understand, that the "intelligible world" is a world of poesy, and that precisely upon this fact rests its worth and nobleness.'[17]

All knowledge is therefore relative. It cannot be founded on any absolute truth, because no such truth can ever be discovered. We can know only what our physical and cognitive organization permits us to know. The truths discovered by the natural sciences are always provisional. They may always be corrected if we come to understand them better or learn to make more accurate observations. (This of course is not a revolutionary statement, but the assumption behind all scientific method since the Scientific Revolution of the seventeenth century.)

Summarizing Lange for his friend Gersdorff, Nietzsche emphasized with particular excitement the conclusion that metaphysical constructs are really conceptual poetry. Philosophy was therefore a form of art. 'Art is free,' he wrote, 'even in the domain of concepts. Who would refute a movement by Beethoven, or charge Raphael's Madonna with a mistake?' (to Gersdorff, end of August 1866). Philosophers should abandon their impossible search for absolute truth and provide something attractive, edifying and ennobling – as in Nietzsche's view Schopenhauer had pre-eminently done.

This approach lands Nietzsche with a philosophical dilemma. Of course one would like a philosophy that is attractive and uplifting, and Schopenhauer's would be better than most. But if one is to live by a philosophy, one wants it not only to be pleasing and uplifting, but to be true – not absolutely true, but as close to truth as the conditions of our knowledge permit. It should be based on convincing arguments yet capable of improvement, just as a scientific theory should be. So philosophy for Nietzsche becomes two things: a glorious realm of freedom where the imagination can devise inspiring fictions, but also the scene of a dogged search for truth – the commitment to truth that was one of the qualities he valued in Schopenhauer. These two goals are not compatible. If you read Nietzsche's work with the first in mind, as many commentators have done in recent decades, you end up with one

Nietzsche; if you read it as a search for truth, you end up with a quite different Nietzsche. Each view can find textual support.

With all this exciting philosophical reading, Nietzsche was beginning to find philology rather dry. One can see why when he responds to a request from Deussen by sending him a list of scholars who have studied the use of the genitive and ablative cases in various Latin authors (to Deussen, 4 April 1867). Two days later he complains to Gersdorff that most philologists are obsessed with petty details: 'For let us not deny it, most philologists lack that uplifting overall view of the ancient world, because they are standing too close to the picture and investigate a speck of oil instead of admiring and – what is more – enjoying the great, bold features of the painting as a whole' (6 April 1867). Eighteen months later, in a letter to Deussen, his distaste for philology has become scurrilous: 'If I am to speak mythologically, I regard philology as a monster born to the goddess Philosophy, sired by an idiot or a cretin' (late October 1868).

In the meantime, a break from philology was provided by Nietzsche's year of compulsory military service, starting in October 1867. He was assigned to an artillery regiment stationed in Naumburg, which meant he could live at home. He worked very hard on improving his riding technique and taking care of his horse, whose name was Balduin; in February 1868 he reported proudly that he was considered the best horseman out of thirty recruits. In March, however, while trying to leap onto Balduin's back, he slipped and fell hard against the stiff pommel of the saddle, tearing two muscles in his chest. The damage was slow to heal, with pus persistently leaking from the wound, and it looked as though part of the breastbone might have to be cut off (an operation performed without anaesthetic, other than the morphine that already served as a painkiller). Fortunately, a medical specialist recommended him instead to take salt-water baths, which ended the inflammation and suppuration. While convalescing, he worked

Nietzsche in Prussian military uniform, 1868.

on compiling an index to Ritschl's journal, a task that dragged on for two years (graduate students, then as now, were liable to have tedious jobs passed on to them by their teachers). He was officially discharged from the army in October 1868.

Just at this time, an overwhelming new figure entered his life. For some time, Nietzsche had been gaining appreciation for Wagner's music, although before the invention of the gramophone opportunities to explore music were limited to live performances. (Although neither man knew it, they were distantly related; genealogists have found a common ancestor in the sixteenth century.) Back in Leipzig, Nietzsche attended an orchestral performance of the overture to *Die Meistersinger* and the prelude to *Tristan* on 27 October 1868. That same evening he wrote to Rohde: 'I cannot bring myself to regard this music with critical coolness; every fibre, every nerve in me is still twitching.' Only a week later, on 6 November, fellow student Ernst Windisch left a note at Nietzsche's lodgings inviting him to meet Wagner in person. Wagner was in Leipzig, his birthplace, incognito, visiting a professor, Hermann Brockhaus, whose wife was a friend of Frau Ritschl. Nietzsche arrived at the Brockhauses' home on the evening of 8 November, having been unable to obtain a dinner suit and hoping that a dark jacket would be acceptable. The evening went swimmingly. Wagner displayed his outsize personality, playing passages from *Die Meistersinger* both before and after dinner and reading out extracts from his autobiography. He was irresistibly charming, asked Nietzsche about himself and, best of all, turned out to be another ardent Schopenhauerian. At the end of the evening, Wagner shook Nietzsche warmly by the hand and invited him to visit so that they could revel in music and philosophy. As Wagner lived in Switzerland, however, a visit seemed a remote prospect.

Two months later, everything changed. Ritschl raised his support for Nietzsche to a higher level by recommending him for the newly vacated chair of classical philology at the Swiss University of Basel. In his reference, Ritschl declared that in 39 years of teaching, he had never encountered a young man who had attained such maturity as early as Nietzsche had. 'He is the idol and (without wishing it) the leader of all the young philologists here in Leipzig,' Ritschl added.[18] Nietzsche was duly offered the post. This was an extraordinary event, although not principally because Nietzsche was only 24. Basel tended to appoint young professors who generally moved on to better-paid posts in Germany: Nietzsche's predecessor, Adolf Kiessling, had been appointed at the age of 25, and his successor, Jacob Wackernagel, would take over Nietzsche's chair in 1879 at the age of 26. The crucial point was that Nietzsche did not have a doctorate, let alone the qualification (*Habilitation*), based on writing a second, longer thesis, which was and is required for a permanent academic appointment in Germany. Leipzig hastily awarded him a doctorate based on the articles he had published in Ritschl's journal.

Naturally Nietzsche leapt at the offer. But he was aware of downsides. The job, which started in April, would involve very hard work preparing lectures and seminars, and in addition he would be required to teach Greek at the Basel Pädagogium (grammar school). He and Rohde had been planning to spend time in Paris studying the natural sciences; that was now impossible. He valued friendship intensely, but in Basel he would be remote from his friends. On the other hand, he would be closer to Wagner, who lived with his partner Cosima (1837–1930), née Liszt, the not-yet-divorced wife of the conductor Hans von Bülow, at Tribschen on Lake Lucerne, only 80 kilometres from Basel.

Basel, where Nietzsche arrived on 19 April 1869, was a small, self-governing city of some 30,000 inhabitants.[19] It was dominated by a number of wealthy merchant families who formed an open elite (rather than a closed patriciate) and dominated the senate and the cabinet. Their outlook was conservative, in that they tried to retain their autonomy by resisting the pressures for centralized government that emanated from Zurich. But it was also liberal enough to provide a secure home for unorthodox scholars: both native Swiss, including the classicist and mythographer Johann Jakob Bachofen (1815–1887) and the historian Jacob Burckhardt (1818–1897, already famous for *The Civilization of the Renaissance in Italy*, 1860), and émigrés from Germany such as Nietzsche and the theologian Franz Overbeck (1837–1905). Its university, founded in 1460, had fallen on hard times, but was strengthened in the mid-nineteenth century by donations from wealthy and public-spirited citizens. It was answerable to the senator responsible for education, Wilhelm Vischer-Bilfinger (1808–1874), who had himself been its professor of Greek from 1835 to 1861, and always gave Nietzsche strong support. It was small, with only 116 students in 1870, the majority being theologians. Nietzsche found that there were only eight students of philology.

Nietzsche threw himself into his duties with energy and success. He had a heavy teaching load: six lectures and a seminar each week, plus six hours teaching senior classes at the

Postcard of Basel, 1928, showing the old university building overlooking the Rhine, with the tower of the Minster in the background.

Pädagogium. At least in such a small city everything was close together: his lodgings, pleasantly situated on the city's edge, were only ten minutes' walk from the Pädagogium on the Münsterplatz (Minster Square) that dominates Basel, and from the university, which at that time was situated on the Rheinsprung, the steep street leading down from the Münsterplatz to the Rhine. Although initially lonely, he soon received rather more social invitations than he wanted. He got to know Bachofen and – much better, although always with a certain distance – Burckhardt, whom he privately considered a 'brilliant eccentric' (to Rohde, 29 May 1869). Nietzsche and Burckhardt often took walks together or met in the cloisters of the Minster, talking about their common interest in Schopenhauer, Greek antiquity and the Italian Renaissance. Burckhardt's conservative distaste for democratic aspirations also strengthened Nietzsche's opposition to what he considered the growth of democracy and liberalism in his time.

In 1870 Nietzsche acquired another lasting friend in Overbeck, appointed at the age of 33 to the chair of New Testament studies and Church history. The two lived in the same house and agreed in opposing the dominant tendencies of their respective academic subjects. While Nietzsche deplored the narrowness of classical philology, Overbeck complained that current theology tended to remove faith from religion and replace it with mere religious knowledge. He would argue this case in a little book, *On the Christian Character of our Present-Day Theology* (1873), which caused a scandal among theologians comparable to that which Nietzsche would provoke in 1872 with *The Birth of Tragedy*.

And of course Nietzsche also visited the Wagners in their lakeside villa at Tribschen. After his first visit on 21 May 1869, he paid four further weekend visits between June and August. He was delighted with the intelligent and gracious Cosima,[20] but, as he shows little interest in animals (apart from the symbolic ones in *Zarathustra*), probably less so by the menagerie which shared

Jacob Burckhardt,
c. 1892.

the Wagner premises, including two dogs, two horses and two peacocks named Wotan and Fricka. After his first visit he wrote Wagner an effusive letter of thanks, hailing him as a genius, and to Rohde he announced: 'Wagner really is all we hoped for: an extravagantly rich and great spirit, an energetic character and an enchantingly amiable person, with the strongest desire for knowledge' (29 May 1869). In return, Nietzsche sometimes went shopping for the Wagners in Basel, even buying silk undergarments to satisfy Wagner's luxurious tastes.

Nietzsche also immersed himself in Wagner's prose writings. In *Art and Revolution* (1849) the fiery young Wagner had maintained that Greek tragedy, dominated by the visionary power conferred by Apollo, presented the Athenians with a supremely beautiful image of their communal life. With the decline of the Greek state, however, tragedy too had declined. Its original unity of acting, music and

Nietzsche with his mother, 1870.

Franz Overbeck, 1876.

words had disintegrated. As an exploration of life's mysteries, it had been superseded by philosophy. The Roman Empire made its subjects into slaves and Christianity filled them with self-contempt. Modern art was commercial. The theatre had split into drama and opera. In *Opera and Drama* (1851) Wagner expressed his ambition to fuse the two in his innovatory music-dramas. Although Wagner's revolutionary zeal had abated since his discovery of Schopenhauer in 1854, and although he condemned the slavery that Nietzsche thought indispensable as the basis of culture, these essays fed into *The Birth of Tragedy* and Nietzsche's later writings.[21]

In summer 1870, to most people's astonishment, France declared war on Prussia. The ostensible issue was that each country was supporting a different candidate for the throne

Richard Wagner and
Cosima Wagner,
née Liszt, 1872,
photograph by Fritz
Luckhardt.

of Spain, but this dispute provided Bismarck, the Prussian
Chancellor, with an opportunity to unite the German states, many
of which were already allied with Prussia in the North German
Confederation, against a common enemy and thus bring about
German unification. Nietzsche, knowing nothing of these political
manoeuvres, fell into a mood of exalted patriotism. He was not
obliged to join up, as he had renounced his Prussian citizenship
on assuming his position in Basel (and, as he did not reside
continuously in Basel for the eight years necessary to claim Swiss
citizenship, he was stateless for the rest of his life). But he told
Vischer-Bilfinger he had to answer Germany's summons and do
his 'German duty' (8 August 1870). The university granted him leave
of absence to serve as a medical orderly. Cosima Wagner pointed

out that Germany didn't need his services: it was not a national emergency; the victorious army was already established on French soil; medical services were as well organized as the army and dilettantes like him would only get in the way. However, Nietzsche, after a two-day training course at Erlangen, marched to occupied France via the battlefield of Wörth, which was strewn with corpses. Having reached the neighbourhood of Metz, he helped to transport wounded men back to a hospital at Karlsruhe in Germany. He then returned to Erlangen and went down with dysentery and diphtheria, thus further burdening the medical services. His war service had lasted a week, but it had taught him how grim war really was, disclosing 'the terrible lower depths of life' (to Gersdorff, 7 November 1870). During that week, the Germans won their decisive victory over the French at Sedan (1–2 September) and captured Emperor Napoleon III. In the aftermath of victory, Wilhelm I of Prussia was declared emperor of a united Germany in the Hall of Mirrors at Versailles.

The consequences of the war filled Nietzsche with dismay. His patriotic outburst had expressed identification with the German cultural nation (as in the anthem the *Deutschlandlied*, which celebrates 'German women, German loyalty, German wine and German song'), not with any political entity, and certainly not with the Prussian-dominated new empire. He called present-day Prussia 'a power extremely dangerous for culture' (to Gersdorff, 7 November 1870), complained to Rohde about the 'awful anti-cultural Prussia' (23 November 1870) and in 1873, in the first of the *Untimely Meditations*, he attacked the illusion that the Prussian victory somehow proved the superiority of German culture. Such an illusion, he warned, could transform the victory into *'the defeat, if not the extirpation of the German spirit for the benefit of the "German Reich"'* (*UM* 3; emphasis in original).

Culture, which was what Nietzsche principally cared about, was threatened from above by the official philistinism of the new

Reich, but also from below by the workers' movement. France's capitulation had prompted in 1871 a working-class insurrection, known as the Commune, that took control of Paris. While resisting the government forces that eventually massacred them, the workers shot hostages, including the Archbishop of Paris, and burned the Tuileries and other public buildings. It was widely believed in Germany that they had destroyed the Louvre with all its paintings and Greek sculptures. The day Nietzsche heard this rumour was, he said, the worst day of his life (to Vischer-Bilfinger, 27 May 1871). He perceived international socialism as a monster, a 'hydra' with many heads, engaged in a 'struggle against culture' (to Gersdorff, 21 June 1871). Nietzsche was convinced that culture depended on maintaining the natural inequality among human beings. The egalitarian goals of socialism must mean the end of culture.

Back in Basel, Nietzsche could not easily reconcile himself to teaching philology. In December 1870 he sent Vischer-Bilfinger an application for a newly vacant chair of philosophy. This was entirely unrealistic. Nietzsche had no formal qualification and no publications in philosophy. His knowledge of philosophy was patchy and much of it second-hand, courtesy of Lange. He knew the pre-Socratics, Plato and of course Schopenhauer, but he had not read such key works as Aristotle's *Metaphysics* and *Ethics*, or Kant's *Critique of Pure Reason*. An irony about his application was that, if it had succeeded, he would have become one of the academic philosophers whom his idol Schopenhauer had denounced in the entertaining polemic 'On University Philosophy' (in *Parerga and Paralipomena*). Naturally nothing came of his request. For the foreseeable future, he had to remain a philologist.

2

The Cultural Critic

There is plenty of philosophy in Nietzsche's first book, *The Birth of Tragedy*. Academics who opened the book expecting a conventional treatise on classical literature were baffled and dismayed. They found instead a brilliant, individual and wayward construction that included a universal theory of aesthetic experience, dependent on Schopenhauer; a revisionist account of the development of Athenian tragedy, of its flourishing in the fifth century BCE and of its decline; a new and surprising account of the Greeks' character and world-view; and a diagnosis of the ills of the modern world along with a prescription for their cure through the rebirth of tragedy in the form of Wagnerian music-drama. All of this was presented not with the sobriety of academic scholarship, but in an urgent, eloquent, often rhapsodical style that at times verged on bombast.

Nietzsche began writing it in spring 1871. Illness, no doubt partly due to overwork, enabled him to obtain two months' leave of absence, which he spent with his sister in Lugano, in the Italian-speaking part of Switzerland. He completed the text during the summer and showed it to the Wagners. In October he submitted the manuscript to Wagner's publisher in Leipzig, E. W. Fritzsch, who accepted it on 16 November and published it, with what now seems amazing celerity, on 29 December, as *The Birth of Tragedy from the Spirit of Music*.

Right at the start Nietzsche puts forward an aesthetic theory that rests on two opposed principles, both grounded in human physiology: 'the opposed artistic worlds of *dream* and *intoxication*'

(*BT* 1). These are in turn aligned with two Greek gods, Apollo and Dionysus. Apollo, the god of light, is associated with the visual arts, in which objects are presented with a visionary clarity resembling that of dreams. Just as the object is distinct and self-contained, so the spectator is clearly separate from the object. In the Dionysian experience, on the other hand, intoxication removes the gulf between the individual and the world around him. All barriers are annulled. In the drug-induced experiences known in all primitive cultures, humanity again becomes one with nature: 'The chariot of Dionysus overflows with flowers and wreaths; beneath its yoke tread the panther and the tiger' (*BT* 1). Transmuted into art, this is the experience of music; Nietzsche illustrates it from the 'Ode to Joy' section of Beethoven's Ninth Symphony, where humanity is urged to feel like a single unit kneeling in the immediate presence of the Creator.

Nietzsche simultaneously presents this opposition in terms drawn from Schopenhauer, who is twice quoted at length (1, 16). Apollo represents the *principium individuationis*, the illusion of being a distinct and separate entity. Dionysus represents the primal unity, 'das Ur-Eine', and hence the knowledge that all things are one and that individuality is a short-lived illusion. The Dionysian experience permits us to look behind the 'veil of Maya' and to feel 'unity with the innermost ground of the world' (2). Apollonian art shows us the variety of objects in the world and allows us to enjoy them; Dionysian art conveys that all these objects are illusory, and expresses this through music: 'music gives the innermost core which preceded all assumption of form, or the heart of things' (16). But to look behind the veil of Maya is not in itself a pleasant experience, for one learns that all individual beings are doomed to destruction. Hence the supreme art form is tragedy, for tragedy centres on the destruction of a person, and not just of anyone, but of a person whose outstanding qualities make him suitable to be the tragic hero. His destruction is painful: Greek myths adapted by tragedians tell how the guilty Oedipus blinded himself and how Prometheus, having defied the gods by helping humankind, was chained to a rock and tormented by an eagle. The hero's tragic fate nevertheless reconciles us to the horror of life by inducing us to feel joy, exultation and acceptance. Such an experience cannot be adequately summed up in words, let alone expressed as a philosophical theory. It can only be felt, and that requires the cooperation of Apollo and Dionysus in tragedy. Apolline art enables us to visualize the hero as a distinct being on the stage; Dionysian music enables us to participate in his downfall, to become momentarily part of the primal unity into which he is reabsorbed, and to rejoice. Thus tragedy provides metaphysical consolation, reassuring us 'that life at the bottom of things, in spite of the passing of phenomena, remains indestructibly powerful and pleasurable' (7).

Nietzsche's account of tragedy differs from the familiar narrative of its development given by Aristotle in the *Poetics*. Aristotle says that tragedy originated from the dithyramb or choric song, but that even Aeschylus, the earliest of the great tragedians, reduced the importance of the chorus, gave the leading role to speech and, instead of a single reciter on the stage, added a second figure and thus made more dramatic interaction possible.[1] In Nietzsche's version, the basic element in tragedy is and remains the chorus. Members of the chorus have already left their individual selves behind and merged into a greater unity: 'This process of the tragic chorus is the original *dramatic* phenomenon: to see oneself transformed before one's very eyes and to act as if one had really entered into another body and another character' (8). The process of self-loss extends to the audience. They are not an audience in the modern sense, that is, they are not detached individual onlookers. Seated in the amphitheatre, where everyone can see everyone else, they each feel that they are part of a greater whole, members of the chorus. They even believe that the actor playing the hero is himself the god Dionysus. And by identifying with the chorus, they identify also with the primal unity which the chorus represents: 'For a few short moments we really are the original essence [*das Urwesen*] itself and feel its unbridled craving for existence and joy in existence; the struggle, the agony, the annihilation of phenomena now seem necessary to us, in the context of the excess of countless forms of existence which crowd and push their way into life, of the overwhelming fertility of the world-will' (17).

And yet Greek tragedy was short-lived. Among its three great tragedians, Aeschylus, Sophocles and Euripides, Nietzsche already finds hints of decline in Sophocles, and Euripides, late in the fifth century, can no longer understand his great predecessors. Two things have gone wrong. First, Euripides has brought the spectator onto the stage, in that he has made concessions to realism that enable the spectator to discover on the stage figures like himself. The inexorability of tragic fate is no longer bearable and is replaced by happy endings, brought about by the intervention of a *deus ex machina*. Music loses its dominance and is used merely to underpin the action and to imitate natural sounds, such as a storm. Second, Euripides regarded himself as primarily a thinker. While the conflicts in earlier tragedies required mystical acceptance, the problems in Euripides require only rational solutions. Visions and ecstasies are now replaced by ideas and emotions.

Moreover, Euripides entered into a fateful alliance with the philosopher Socrates. Socrates had an optimistic, anti-tragic outlook. He thought that to act rightly, you had first to know what was right and then do it; bad actions were errors resulting from ignorance. He disapproved of all art forms except Aesop's fables, which taught useful lessons. In contrast to the 'tragic man', who submits wordlessly to what is rationally incomprehensible, Socrates typifies the 'theoretical man', for whom life consists of problems to be understood and solved rationally.

Socrates' influence extends to the present day. The modern world is enmeshed in 'Socratic' or 'Alexandrian' culture (18;

alluding to the ancient Library of Alexandria, and thus to bookishness). Music now often takes the form of opera, in which it is subordinate to the words; this is especially obvious in the recitative, a mere 'half-song' (19) in which the singer restrains himself to ensure that the words can be understood. We do not understand the Greeks of the tragic age. Modern scholars speak patronizingly of their serenity (*Heiterkeit*). Our universities approach them either via tedious textual editing, or via historical scholarship which places them in a remote and irrelevant past.

Socratism has brought about a wider crisis. Its modern devotees ignore what Nietzsche takes to be obvious, that high culture requires the existence of a leisured class maintained by slaves: 'in its optimistic view of existence, it denies the necessity of such a class and therefore, when the effect of its beautiful words of seduction and reassurance about the "dignity of man" and the "dignity of labour" is exhausted, it gradually drifts towards its end in horrific annihilation' (18). Such optimism has allowed the modern work force to become 'a barbaric slave-class' (18) which is now bent on revenge; the supposed 'noble savage' is now demanding his rights, supported by 'the present socialistic movement' (19). Yet, and this is Nietzsche's message for the present, there are signs of hope. The exhaustion of the Socratic culture of knowledge is revealed by Goethe's Faust, who has run through all the learning available in his day and longs for more satisfying experiences. German philosophy, represented by Kant and Schopenhauer, confirms that the world is not fully intelligible to the rational mind; for Kant, reality is the inaccessible *Ding an sich*, which Schopenhauer reinterprets as the metaphysical Will. German music has already established a great tradition, running from Bach via Beethoven to Wagner. Wagner above all, as Nietzsche shows in an appreciation of *Tristan und Isolde*, has restored music to the dominant position in his music-dramas. Moreover, Wagner is able to satisfy the modern hunger for myth. Every culture needs a myth in which its understanding of the world is translated into narratives and images. Modern versions of Christianity have lost touch with their original myth and now appeal only to scholars. Nietzsche prophesies an imminent rebirth of tragic culture.

This tragic culture will be specifically German. German music and German philosophy have converged to lay its foundations. Since one cannot borrow myths from another people, the myths it relies on will be Germanic, and towards the end of his treatise Nietzsche makes many allusions to the myths underpinning Wagner's *Ring des Nibelungen*, which would have its premiere at Bayreuth in 1876:

> Let no one believe that the German spirit has lost its mythical home for all eternity, when it can still understand so clearly the birdsong which tells it of that home. One day it will awaken in the morning freshness which follows a great sleep: then it will slay dragons, annihilate the spiteful dwarfs, and awaken Brünnhilde – and Wotan's spear itself will not be able to bar its way! (24)

Nietzsche's celebration of German culture goes even further. He looks forward to the excision of all 'Romance' (that is, French) elements. This German rebirth will be a counterpart to the Reformation three centuries earlier, which began with Luther's revolt against the papacy. It will be encouraged by Germany's victory over France in 'the courageous triumph and bloody glory of the recent war' (23). How a new German tragic culture is meant to avert the destruction planned by socialists is not spelled out, but these emphatic political messages will find echoes in Nietzsche's later writings, although his attachment to Germany will presently swing round into an unsparing rejection, eventually including even Wagner.

After all this it feels a little pedantic to ask how far Nietzsche's account of the origin of tragedy is true. He himself seems insecure about his argument, for he admits that the overwhelming effect he ascribes to Greek tragedy cannot be inferred from its words, which are the only form in which tragedy survives. The musical effect has to be reconstructed 'in an almost scholarly manner' (17). And although Nietzsche does not say what materials can serve towards this reconstruction, and indeed goes into remarkably little detail about Greek music, he seems fatally to undermine his own case by adding that 'in the whole development of Greek music – compared with the infinitely richer music which we know and are familiar with – we believe that we hear only the opening notes of the youthful song of musical genius intoned with a timid sense of power' (17).

Classical scholars have listed *The Birth of Tragedy*'s weaknesses, but also acknowledged its strengths.[2] The core argument about the origin of tragedy from the amalgamation of Apollonian and Dionysian forces cannot be demonstrated. It was in any case Apollo, not Dionysus, whom the Greeks regarded as the god of music. The Greeks had a limited range of musical instruments – 'flutes', really pipes played in the manner of a modern clarinet, and a range of stringed instruments collectively called 'lyres' – and no harmony, counterpoint or polyphony; on the Greek stage music was subordinate to the word, just as Nietzsche complains of in modern opera. In talking about Greek music, Nietzsche seems to be projecting Wagnerian music-theatre back onto classical Athens. Further, there was no alliance between Euripides and Socrates, who were twenty years apart in age. Yet classical scholars admit that the book eventually had a powerful influence by revealing the centrality of religion in Greek culture. It inspired Nietzsche's friend Rohde to write his important book *Psyche* (1894) on Greek beliefs concerning immortality.[3] Even Nietzsche's account of Greek dreams finds confirmation from the classical scholar E. R. Dodds, who in his famous book on the irrational side of Greek life notes that the Greeks never spoke of having a dream but of 'seeing a dream'.[4]

The Birth of Tragedy was a challenge to the narrow outlook that Nietzsche condemned in philology, and an attempt to provide a broad picture of Greek culture and an insight into the spirit animating it. In its reliance on philosophy, it was also a slap in the face for Nietzsche's teacher Ritschl. It was perhaps not surprising that the book was denounced by most colleagues. An eminent professor in Bonn was reported to have told his students that anyone who could write such nonsense was 'dead to scholarship' (to Rohde, 25 October 1872). The 23-year-old Ulrich von Wilamowitz (1848–1931), who had been four years behind Nietzsche at Pforta and would grow into a classical scholar of the first eminence, attacked the book in a pamphlet entitled 'Philology of the Future!' ('Zukunftsphilologie!', an allusion to Wagner's term *Zukunftsmusik*, 'music of the future'). This pamphlet, full of nasty personal invective, received a reply from Rohde, who showed, in a proper scholarly manner, that Wilamowitz had often misquoted and misrepresented Nietzsche. Wilamowitz illustrated the obtuseness of his profession. And yet, Nietzsche maintained, all the criticisms of *The Birth of Tragedy* rested on a misunderstanding: although philologists could learn much from his book, 'I was not writing for philologists' (to Malwida von Meysenbug, 7 November 1872). Eventually *The Birth of Tragedy* would reach the general reader and prove to be one of the most popular and inspiring of Nietzsche's works.

The book was praised in particular by Burckhardt, to whom Nietzsche was in some measure indebted for his understanding of Greek culture.[5] Burckhardt was already famous for his book on the Italian Renaissance. Nietzsche attended Burckhardt's lectures on the study of history in autumn 1870, as well as those on Greek civilization, which began in the winter term of 1872 and attracted an audience of 54 matriculated students (almost half the student body) along with several visitors from the town.[6] Burckhardt's study of ancient Greece, published only posthumously, explores the positive value of strife and competition, especially in the sixth century BCE, which he calls the Agonal Age.[7] He reinforced not only Nietzsche's understanding of Greece but the anti-modern

views that accompanied it. He gives a very unattractive account
of Athenian democracy, comparing it to the Reign of Terror in
the French Revolution, and attributing to it the decline of Athens.
In his own time Burckhardt was unsympathetic to the growth
of liberalism and democracy in Switzerland: 'I know too much
history to expect this despotism of the masses to lead to anything
but a future rule by violence.'[8] Regarding both Greece and modern
Europe, therefore, Burckhardt helped Nietzsche to develop radical
views – although Nietzsche far outdid his mentor.

The Greeks as Alien

Nietzsche's early writings continually emphasize the *alterity* of the
Greeks. Greek culture was utterly different from that of modern
Europe. According to Nietzsche, we are still so much influenced by
Christianity that it is hard to grasp how different the Greeks were,
and our educational system adds to the difficulty by pretending
that Greek culture is in some way the ancestor of ours. Nietzsche
explodes such mistakes not only in *The Birth of Tragedy* but in two
trenchant essays which he did not publish, 'The Greek State' and
'Homer's Contest'. At the end of 1872 Nietzsche wrote them out,
along with three other essays, had them bound in leather and sent
them as a present to Cosima Wagner under the collective title
'Five Prefaces to Five Unwritten Books'. Together with *The Birth
of Tragedy*, and often more drastically, they compose a picture of
Greek culture as alien, in some ways repugnant, and thus a counter-
image to modern cultural values.

Anyone who approaches Greek religion with expectations derived
from Christianity will be baffled by encountering a completely
alien religious sensibility. The Greek gods do not offer love, mercy,
morality or disembodied spirituality. Imagined as corporeal and
joyous, continually feasting on Mount Olympus, they represent
an affirmation of life. But this affirmation has nothing to do with

the 'serenity' that Nietzsche's academic contemporaries commonly ascribed to the Greeks. It was the counterpart to the profound pessimism which Nietzsche illustrates with the legendary statement by the wise satyr Silenus that the best thing for mortals was 'not to have been born, not to *be*, to be *nothing*. But the second best thing for you is – to meet an early death' (*BT* 3). Nietzsche's example could be supplemented by the chorus in Sophocles' *Oedipus at Colonus*:

> Say what you will, the greatest boon is not to be;
> But, life begun, soonest to end is best
> And to that bourne from which our life began
> Swiftly return.[9]

Theognis, the author about whom Nietzsche wrote his first learned article, expresses a similar sentiment: 'It is best for all mortals not to be born and not to look upon the rays of the piercing sun, but once born it is best to pass under the gates of Hades as quickly as possible and to lie under a large heap of earth.'[10]

The Greeks, according to Nietzsche, were profoundly pessimistic: 'The Greek knew and felt the terrors and horrors of existence' (*BT* 3). It was not only that survival in a subsistence economy required constant labour from all but a privileged few, and that Greek states often waged wars which centred on hand-to-hand combat and had a high death rate. Life itself rested on destruction. Greek myths are full of cannibalism, castration, dismemberment and murder within families. The most famous myths, used by tragedians, are about appalling punishments imposed on mortals for their crimes against the gods. Oedipus, the wisest of men, solved the Sphinx's riddle, but as implicit punishment for his more than human knowledge he was led into committing parricide and incest. Prometheus defied the gods by stealing fire from heaven and giving it to mortals, thereby making human civilization possible, but for this crime he was chained to a mountain peak and condemned to have his liver torn out every day by an eagle.

This leads Nietzsche to maintain, in a curious digression, that the Greeks exemplify the essentially masculine and Aryan concept of crime (*Frevel*), whereas the myth of the Fall of Man resulting from Eve's curiosity illustrates the essentially feminine and Semitic concept of sin (*BT* 9). Behind this idiosyncratic speculation lies the nineteenth-century tendency to argue rashly from linguistic to racial distinctions. The 'Aryan' (we would now say 'Indo-European') and 'Semitic' language families had been identified late in the previous century. It seemed obvious that these distinctions must correspond to cultural and psychological differences between 'races'. Nietzsche's speculation here, however, appears to be his own. It is marginal to his argument in *The Birth of Tragedy*, and is not developed in later writings, even where he mentions the 'Aryan race' (*GM* I 5).

Being acutely aware of the horror of life, the Greeks, in order to go on living, conjured up the contrasting image of Mount Olympus. The image of the eternally happy gods made human life seem worth living. The hideous abyss of reality was concealed behind art: 'for only as an *aesthetic spectacle* are existence and the world *justified* to eternity' (*BT* 5). They were thus able to live with the awareness that life is profoundly cruel: 'Every moment devours the one before it, every birth is the death of innumerable beings. Procreation, life and murder are all one' ('State', 768).

That being so, the Greeks accepted that the cruelty of life should be replicated in the structure of society. The natural condition of life was a Hobbesian *bellum omnium contra omnes* ('State', 772). This anarchy could only be brought under control by a powerful state imposed violently by conquerors. The exercise of power, Nietzsche says, is always evil, but it was and is necessary. Modern humanitarians, socialists and liberals are mere hypocrites: they promote loyalty to the modern state, refusing to admit that it is an instrument of domination, and they bamboozle the labouring masses with slogans like 'human dignity', 'the dignity of labour' and 'equal rights'. The Greeks were frank in considering manual labour disgraceful and in compelling people to do it by force. Modern wage-slaves are no better off than ancient labourers who were acknowledged as slaves, and much worse off than medieval serfs: 'How elevating it is to contemplate the medieval serf, connected by powerful and delicate legal and moral relationships to his social superior, and with his own existence enclosed in profound peace – how elevating – and what a reproach!' ('State', 769).[11]

Unencumbered by illusions or delusions about power, the Greeks were the most political people who ever existed, apart perhaps from the men of the Italian Renaissance (Nietzsche is doubtless thinking especially of the soberly amoral analyses of power presented by Machiavelli). The small leisured elite were constantly occupied with politics. Their violent impulses were unleashed in internecine political struggles and in wars against other states: 'this bloody jealousy of city against city, of party against party, the murderous greed of these petty wars, the tiger-like triumphing over the corpse of the vanquished enemy, in short, the perpetual recollection of those scenes of battle and atrocity which we see Homer, as a true Hellene, contemplating with pleasurable absorption' ('State', 771). War, however, is not in itself a bad thing. At the present day, international peace is being sought most eagerly by financiers who want to manipulate the state for their own ends, a 'selfish, stateless aristocracy of money' ('State', 774). War disrupts the power of such people, and is thus, like slavery, unattractive but useful to society.

If society has any purpose, it is to foster genius. Danger and insecurity are conducive to genius; prolonged peace merely promotes mediocrity. Greek genius flourished in the intervals between wars. Plato imagined an ideal society ruled by an elite of geniuses, although unfortunately the bad influence of Socrates made him want to banish artists and allow only philosophical geniuses. Warfare promotes military genius, and the military genius (such as Alexander the Great, but one thinks also of Napoleon) is entitled to deploy and destroy vast numbers of men in pursuit of his plans. In doing so, he confers on them the only dignity they can possibly have, for, contrary to modern egalitarianism, '"man in himself", absolute man, has neither dignity, nor rights, nor duties: it is only as a being who unconsciously obeys fully determined purposes that man can excuse his existence' ('State', 776).

Genius was developed in Greece by means wholly antithetical to Christian morality. Christianity urges us to suppress our bad passions. The Greeks indulged their passions of cruelty, envy and hatred, showing 'tiger-like pleasure in destruction' ('Contest', 783). They relished the lurid descriptions of battles and deaths in the *Iliad*. In actual warfare they routinely practised atrocities. When a city was conquered, the men would be massacred, the women and children sold into slavery.[12]

These passions, however, were channelled into cultural achievement by encouraging envy. Nietzsche tells how, according to the poet Hesiod, the goddess of strife, Eris, was really twofold. There is one Eris who 'fosters evil; war and conflict – cruel one, no mortal loves that one'; but also another, who rouses people to work:

> For a man who is not working but who looks at some other man, a rich one who is hastening to plow and plant and set his house in order, he envies him, one neighbor envying his neighbor who is hastening towards wealth: and this Strife is good for mortals. And potter is angry with potter, and builder with builder, and beggar begrudges beggar, and poet poet.[13]

This mutual envy and enmity is the basis of competition, institutionalized as the *agon*. All achievement for the Greeks was competitive. Sportsmen competed at the Olympic Games; tragedians competed for the annual prize; poets competed with the dead by trying to outdo Homer. Competition was the Greeks' way of channelling the force of envy, which would otherwise have been purely destructive. For this to work, however, it was necessary that no one should emerge as the unchallengeable and supreme victor. There always had to be several champions who contended against each other. Nietzsche maintains that ostracism, or banishment, had the purpose of getting rid of anyone who made competition pointless by his excellence.

Nietzsche thus envisages ancient Greece as wholly antithetical to the humanitarian and egalitarian tendencies he observes in modern Europe. The Greeks were dedicated to the pursuit of excellence in the arts, in sport, in physical and intellectual training. Their achievements positively required not just inequality, but injustice and cruelty, the indispensable foundations of high culture. Having said this as an aside in *The Birth of Tragedy* (18), Nietzsche now spells it out unmistakably:

> We must be prepared to assert, as a cruel-sounding truth, that *the essence of a culture requires slavery*: a truth, indeed, that permits no doubt as to the absolute value of existence [. . .] The misery of people who live by toil must be increased yet further in order to enable a small number of Olympian people to produce culture. Here is the source of the enmity that the Communists and Socialists and their paler descendants, the white race of 'liberals', have always nourished against the arts and against classical antiquity. ('State', 767–8)

If culture depended on the will of the people, then it would be extinguished by compassion and a demand for justice. Early Christianity put forward such demands. But it is useless to appeal to religion, for religion, once it attains power, also depends on cruelty, which is inseparable from power. All power, Nietzsche says bluntly, is evil. To have culture, you must accept evil: that is the primal contradiction at the heart of life. And culture is necessary, because it is art alone that makes life worth living. The world becomes endurable only if you see it as a work of art – an insight that Nietzsche has already slipped into *The Birth of Tragedy* (5): 'only as an *aesthetic phenomenon* is existence and the world eternally *justified.*'

How Not to Study the Classics

Even in the degenerate modern world, Nietzsche thought improvements were possible. He hoped that Wagner's theatre in Bayreuth, due to open in 1876, would inspire a renewed German culture. He also thought it possible to bring about reforms in grammar-school and university education. Between January and March 1872 Nietzsche delivered five public lectures on education to an audience of some three hundred in the auditorium of the museum at Basel. The lectures, entitled 'On the Future of our Educational Institutions', were well received, although Nietzsche abandoned his initial plans to publish them.

Some key words in these lectures lack a precise equivalent in English. 'Educational institutions' is an inadequate and misleading translation of *Bildungsanstalten*. No English term has the same range or emotional weight as *Bildung*, which implies 'a general acculturation that may or may not be achieved through formal institutions', including personal cultivation as well as learning.[14] The transmission of *Bildung*, over and above the acquisition of knowledge, was the declared aim of the grammar schools, or *Gymnasien*, which were set up by Wilhelm von Humboldt as minister of education in Prussia (1809–10) and subsequently copied in other German states and Switzerland. Their curriculum focused on the intensive study of the Latin and Greek languages and literature. Like the Renaissance humanists who rediscovered classical texts, Humboldt believed that ancient literature, read in the original languages, was the best guide to humane values.

Hence at Pforta, admittedly a school with an exceptional academic reputation, Nietzsche's education was dominated by Latin and Greek. Science and modern languages were the domain of the vocational schools, or *Realschulen*. Admission to university was reserved for alumni of the *Gymnasien*.

Nietzsche's central contention is that neither *Gymnasien* nor universities any longer transmit *Bildung*, and hence that there are no longer (or not yet) any true *Bildungsanstalten*. He concedes that the *Gymnasien* do teach Latin and Greek grammar properly. But they do not foster reverence for or understanding of classical culture. Instead of *Bildung*, they inculcate learning (*Wissenschaft*). Schoolboys are taught everything about the Greeks except why they matter.

Instruction in German is also inadequate. The foundation of all subsequent education is the ability to write and speak one's mother tongue correctly. Without strict training, young men learn only to write in journalese and fail to develop sensitivity to style. So-called 'classical *Bildung*' is a sham. The classic German writers who really did absorb the spirit of the ancients, such as Schiller, Goethe and Winckelmann, are treated without due respect; they should be used as a bridge from the modern world to a true understanding of the ancients, but this opportunity is not taken. The core of German lessons is the 'German essay', in which the pupil is supposed to express his individuality and develop his own opinions, whereas education ought to teach the immature to bow to authority: 'a proper education will devote all its energy solely to suppressing the ridiculous claim to independence of judgement and will accustom the young person to strict obedience beneath the sceptre of genius' (*zb* 680).

At the universities, the much-lauded principle of 'academic freedom', the liberty to study what one pleases, merely bewilders students, because they have not been trained in their discipline at school. Unable to use their opportunities or to find their way through the vast field of available learning, they fall back on narrow specialisms. If they try to study philosophy, they will find that academic philosophers no longer address the big questions but confine themselves to the minute interpretation of philosophical texts. As for the arts, the university takes no interest in them. The 'historical approach' places the subjects of study firmly in the past and denies them any living relationship to the present. When young men graduate, they go into a profession or, all too often, into journalism, but remain frustrated by the obscure awareness that nobody has tried to bring out their potential, and the result may well be a disappointed resentment against true culture.

Attempts are made to extend this non-education more widely, the modish term being *Volksbildung* or 'popular *Bildung*'. But there can be no such thing; the very word is a contradiction. 'To impart *Bildung* to the masses cannot be our aim; rather, to impart *Bildung* to the select few who are equipped for great and lasting works' (*zb* 698). Although Nietzsche respects the role of the *Realschulen* in providing vocational education, he asserts that the great majority of the population has no concern with *Bildung* but should remain in a 'healthy sleep', providing the soil which is essential to the flourishing of genius. As for those who, wanting to rouse the masses from their slumbers, make delusive promises of *Bildung*, Nietzsche drops dark hints about the real designs of such people. His meaning is explicit in his notebooks: 'Universal *Bildung* is only a preliminary stage of Communism' (*ksa vii* 243). No doubt his audience in 1872, aware of the recent suppression of the Paris Commune, understood what he meant.

The demand for popular education, and for the expansion of universities and schools, comes from the state. Modern states, with Prussia in the vanguard, want a large staff of educated administrators (and it must be remembered that in German-speaking countries not only civil servants but many other professionals, including school and university teachers, are state officials). Hence it drives the demand for ever more *Bildung* while depressing the quality of *Bildung*, for the state only wants capable mediocrities, not men of genius:

> because the genuine German spirit is hated, because the aristocratic nature of true *Bildung* inspires fear, because the aim is to drive the great individuals into exile by sowing and nourishing the pretension to *Bildung* among the masses, because the aim is to escape the hard and rigorous discipline [*Zucht*] of great leaders by persuading the masses that they will find the way themselves – under the guidance of the state! (*ZB* 710)

Nietzsche's lectures thus centre, like *The Birth of Tragedy*, on an attempt to rescue the true German spirit – shown in Luther's Reformation, in German music and philosophy, in the courage of German troops in the recent war – from the degradation of German culture in the newly established Reich. In place of the now prevalent mediocrity, he wants a real *Bildungsanstalt*, a demanding school for the production of geniuses. Only a few people can be geniuses, but a much larger number of people can find a worthy role in supporting them; it is the latter people who are being most seriously misled by the false claim that *Bildung* is potentially available to all.

Untimely Meditations

Over the next few years Nietzsche published a series of long essays under the umbrella title *Untimely Meditations*. He meant to write thirteen of them, but in the event published only four. The last, a eulogy of Wagner, too much resembles advertising copy for Bayreuth, but the first three deserve detailed examination. Although the *Meditations* range widely, they all turn on the question of education, *Bildung* and the survival of German culture.

The first essay is a merciless evisceration of a new and highly popular book by the theologian David Strauss (1808–1874), *The*

Old Faith and the New (1872). Nietzsche was motivated partly by loyalty to Wagner, who had clashed with Strauss in print five years earlier. Strauss had become notorious with his *Life of Jesus Critically Examined* (1835–6), a classic of biblical scholarship, which was translated into English by Marian Evans (George Eliot). His last book is not in the same league. It is a compendium of 'the modern outlook', taking in religion, science, culture and various social issues, for the benefit of middle-class readers. Religion is examined only to be dismissed. Strauss places his faith in Darwin. Although there is no God, Strauss is confident that the universe is rational and good, and that progress is a law of nature. He claims that war is natural and can never be abolished; defends the recent Franco-Prussian War; decries socialism as destructive, instancing the Paris Commune, and condemns the workers' movement as a mere assault on private property; and gives his views on German

David Strauss,
c. 1870.

classical literature and music. He says a good deal that, in the abstract, Nietzsche would have agreed with, but the cocksure tone is repellent, as are his frequent lapses into vulgarity, such as calling the Resurrection 'a world-historical humbug'.

Strauss's book was an instant best-seller, going, as Nietzsche notes, through six impressions within a year of its publication. It took courage to denounce a work idolized by the *bien-pensants* and to demonstrate in detail its intellectual and stylistic incoherence. He was helped by his close friendship with the theologian Overbeck, who for some time lived in the same house as Nietzsche. Overbeck acknowledges Nietzsche's help with his polemic against contemporary trends in theology, *On the Christianity of Our Current Theology* (1873), which includes a critique of Strauss's book. While Overbeck deplores Strauss's meagre conception of Christianity and mocks his 'cult of the universe', Nietzsche attacks his view of culture.[15] In attacking Strauss, Nietzsche is also attacking the self-styled culture of Imperial Germany. He warns (as we have seen) that the triumphalist national mood following the defeat of France is in danger of leading to the extirpation of the German spirit. Thus the Strauss polemic introduces a theme that will run throughout Nietzsche's works: his rejection of the hollow, vulgar, militaristic and chauvinist Imperial Germany.

Strauss, in Nietzsche's opinion, exemplifies a new and deplorable type. He is not just a philistine – a word, as Nietzsche explains, taken from student slang, where it denotes 'the town' as opposed to 'the gown', implying that students are the biblical chosen people and the townspeople are hostile heathen tribes. Rather, he is a philistine who, in his own opinion, has acquired *Bildung* and is thus qualified to pronounce on intellectual issues, philosophy and the arts – a *Bildungsphilister*. Nietzsche underpins this judgement by quoting derisively a great many of Strauss's literary and musical opinions. But Strauss is not just banal: his complacent and condescending comments show no understanding of how Lessing, Goethe and other great German writers had to struggle against an uncomprehending and often hostile world composed of people like Strauss.

In philosophy, Strauss is equally shallow. His claim that the world is rational reminds Nietzsche of Hegel's identification of the rational with the real, which amounts to mere 'worship of success'. His Darwinism is inconsistent, for he adjures his readers to remember that they are human and not mere natural beings. Yet Darwin has shown that we *are* natural beings, that there is no boundary separating humans from other animals. This is a fundamental assumption behind all Nietzsche's work, but it passes Strauss by, for he does not see that Darwinism puts paid to all conventional morality.

Thinking himself an exponent of German culture, Strauss inadvertently reveals that present-day Germany has no culture. Culture, in Nietzsche's view, is something quite different from mere knowledge:

> Culture is above all unity of artistic style in all expressions
> of a nation's life. To know and have learnt a great deal is,
> however, neither a necessary means of attaining culture, nor
> a sign of its presence, and can be perfectly compatible with
> the antithesis of culture – barbarism, that is, the absence
> of style or the chaotic medley of all styles. (*UM* 163)

Nietzsche is presumably thinking of classical Athens, when patterns of behaviour, writing, thought and political life can be seen in retrospect as all of a piece. By contrast, the modern world, thanks to travel and historical research, has access to all past and present cultures, and borrows from them indiscriminately, as a substitute for having a distinctive style of its own. Thus neo-Gothic, neo-Renaissance, neo-Baroque and neo-classical buildings may all stand side by side in the same street.[16]

The Strauss essay gave Nietzsche the opportunity to formulate ideas that would be of lasting importance for him. It is an incisive statement of the antipathy to the new German Reich that would accompany him throughout the rest of his life and eventually be extended back into German history, when Nietzsche blames Luther for cutting short the Renaissance. It is also a brilliant polemic, exposing not only the complacency and timidity of Strauss's thinking but, hilariously, the clumsiness of his style, with its absurd mixed metaphors and lapses of tone and taste. By contrast, Nietzsche here and elsewhere shows himself a master of prose style.

The second *Meditation*, 'On the Use and Disadvantage of History for Life' (1874), asks what the study of history can contribute to *Bildung*. Historical research was among the great achievements of nineteenth-century German culture. Its chief exemplar was the hugely prolific Leopold von Ranke (1795–1886), a pioneer of document-based history whose much-misunderstood ambition was to tell history 'as it actually was', that is, to establish on the basis of evidence what actually happened and to avoid imposing a religious or philosophical interpretation on the facts. Nietzsche mentions with particular respect the classical historian Barthold Georg Niebuhr (1776–1831) and his own Basel friend Burckhardt. He has no intention of disparaging history or historical research as such.

However, history is not just an academic subject. Nietzsche points out various ways in which history enters ordinary life. It is possible to ignore history altogether and live in the moment, as animals do. When in love, or inspired by a noble cause, people do not reflect on the past but concentrate on the present. Such an attitude is 'unhistorical'. Conversely, with enough knowledge, one can adopt a 'supra-historical' standpoint and survey history as a parade of identical passions under different guises. Nietzsche illustrates this attitude from Niebuhr, who speaks of it serenely, and the poet Giacomo Leopardi (1798–1837), for whom it makes all endeavour seem pointless. Or one can think historically in the sense of seeing history as a process whose meaning will eventually be revealed – a view, however, that will end in disappointment.

In ordinary life, history can sustain people in various ways. Monumental history provides us with inspiring past models (Churchill has often fulfilled this role in contemporary Britain). Antiquarian history (a term Nietzsche does not mean disparagingly) looks to the past with affection and reverence (one might imagine someone who, passing the old buildings in his home town – the town hall, churches, a surviving medieval gateway – feels that their presence makes life more stable and supports efforts to conserve them). But both these attitudes have drawbacks. Respect for past models may encourage a selective view of them that ignores their faults. The antiquarian may want to preserve anything old for its own sake and be hostile to any innovation. So both need to be balanced by critical history, which judges the past in accordance with the needs of the present (one might think nowadays of attitudes to past colonial empires). Sometimes the old has to be demolished to make way for the new.

All three standpoints represent ways in which history serves life. For them, history is not an academic subject, but part of the framework in which one lives. In present-day Germany, however, history has become primarily the academic study of history, to such an extent that German culture is weakened and damaged. Academic history, as Nietzsche complained in 'On the Future of our Educational Institutions', denies history any living relationship with the present. Its students, like their colleagues at German universities, do not acquire *Bildung*, but only 'knowledge about *Bildung*'. They swallow huge quantities of facts that they can do nothing with, and which seem to rattle inside them as though they had swallowed stones. An ancient Greek, transported to the present, would have considered them not so much human beings as walking encyclopedias. Here Nietzsche widens his perspective to a polemic against modern culture, or the lack of it. If culture implies unity, modern humanity is fragmented, because our inside does not match our outside. We train our minds, or at least fill them, but we do not cultivate our bodies or devote attention to our appearance.

Nietzsche then enumerates the ill effects of excessive historical study. First, it creates weak personalities, fostering the conformism that is characteristic of modern life: 'Historical education [*Bildung*] and the identical bourgeois coat rule at the same time' (*UM* 84). If modern students study philosophy, it becomes a mere record of what people have thought in the past, with no implications for how one should live one's life now. Without a passionate interest in their studies, students do not care what they specialize in: someone who studies Democritus, the 'laughing philosopher', might just as well be studying his antithesis Heraclitus, the 'weeping philosopher' – who cares?

Nietzsche then addresses the concept of historical objectivity. It ought presumably to mean the ability to judge fairly and dispassionately. But such an ability is a rare virtue that can be attained only by prolonged and rigorous self-discipline. Most practitioners only achieve tolerance, or the power to recount history in a non-judgemental way. But that again is a sign of weakness and indifference. There is no merit in being 'objective' about things you do not care about. In any case, it has little to do with the true objectivity shown by the artist, who cares intensely about his work and is so absorbed in it that no personal considerations can creep in. And, in thinking about the past, why do we need to judge it? Our dealings with the past must be determined by the needs and energies of the present. What the past tells us always has an oracular obscurity: 'only if you are an architect of the future and know the present will you understand it' (*UM* 94).

Historical knowledge can also be destructive. The historical study of religion tends to dissipate the reverent aura which surrounds sacred narratives. If we know too much about the history of Christianity, we end up with 'knowledge about Christianity' instead of Christianity itself (as Overbeck complained). Similarly, one can know too much about works of art. To exert a vital force, religion and art require an atmosphere of mystery. If they are made too accessible, they become unimpressive. This leads Nietzsche into a further critique of modern scholarship, which has come to resemble a factory, the workers being effectively slaves dependent on the academic labour market (all these metaphors, so familiar at the present day, were evidently established by the 1870s).

Yet another disadvantage of the historical sense is the feeling that one is a latecomer, an epigone; that everything worthwhile has already been accomplished, leaving nothing for us to do. If we accept the common comparison of history to the course of a life, we may even imagine that we have reached maturity and have nothing ahead of us but senility. Some people are attracted by the Hegelian conception of a 'world process' that is approaching its consummation. Among these is Eduard von Hartmann (1842–1906), a prominent philosopher of Nietzsche's day, whom Nietzsche mocks almost as mercilessly as he earlier mocked Strauss. To think that we have now attained the high point of history, the peak of a development stretching back through organic evolution from the protozoic slime, is madness. 'Overproud European of the nineteenth century, you are raving!' exclaims Nietzsche (UM 108).

In Nietzsche's view, any teleological view of history is mistaken. History is not a process with a goal: 'No, the goal of humanity cannot lie in its end, but only in its highest exemplars' (UM 111). That is, the 'purpose' of history is to bring forth 'great men' (Nietzsche writes 'grosse Männer', meaning males, not 'Menschen', human beings irrespective of gender), such as Alexander the Great or Raphael. Nietzsche dismisses any idea that history should be concerned with the masses, and hence take a sociological turn. 'The masses seem to me to deserve notice in three respects only: first as faded copies of great men [. . .], then as a force of resistance to great men, finally as instruments in the hands of great men; for the rest, let the Devil and statistics take them!' (*UM* 113).

Nietzsche rejects pessimism about history. If we are latecomers, that can be turned round and interpreted positively: we can inherit the achievements of our predecessors, as the Renaissance did those of antiquity, thus laying the foundation for a new culture. Above all, Nietzsche places his hopes in the fresh, spontaneous, taboo-breaking energies of young people, if they can be saved from the mind-numbing effects of academic study. After all, our present situation is not unique. Our so-called culture may be a bewildering medley of styles and ideas drawn from every land and clime explored by the historical sense. But so was pre-classical Greece. The early Greeks accepted influences from Egypt, Babylon, the entire Near East, but they gradually learned to organize this chaos, to weld its components into something new and homogeneous, the classical culture that made them the model for all subsequent culture. So Nietzsche does not abandon hope for a renewal of German culture 'as a unanimity of life, thought, appearance and will' (*UM* 123).

The meditation entitled 'Schopenhauer as Educator' pays tribute to Schopenhauer as a guide amid this cultural chaos. Nietzsche sums up what a philosopher must consider the dire state of the modern world:

When he thinks of the haste and hurry now universal, of the increasing velocity of life, of the cessation of all contemplativeness and simplicity, he almost thinks that what he is seeing are the symptoms of a total extermination and uprooting of culture. The waters of religion are ebbing away and leaving behind swamps or stagnant pools, the nations are again drawing away from one another in the most hostile fashion and long to tear one another to pieces. The sciences, pursued without any restraint and in the spirit of the blindest *laissez faire*, are shattering and dissolving all firmly held belief; the educated classes and states are being swept along by a hugely contemptible money economy. The world has never been more worldly, never poorer in love and goodness. The educated classes are no longer lighthouses or refuges in the midst of this turmoil of secularization, amid all this restless worldliness; they themselves grow daily more restless, thoughtless and loveless. Everything, contemporary art and science included, serves the coming barbarism. (*UM* 148)

There is no place for real philosophy here. Philosophers nowadays are professors, hence state officials. They pursue truth no further than the state permits, and agree in glorifying the state as the highest human achievement. To them, philosophy is not a vocation but merely a job. Worse still, Germany is and has long been hostile to genius. Beethoven, Goethe, Schopenhauer and Wagner required iron constitutions to fight against the forces that were trying to drag them down. Less robust geniuses, such as the poet Hölderlin and the dramatist Kleist, were broken by this struggle, ending respectively in madness and suicide.

True culture, however, is the attempt to reach an ideal that one apprehends far above one. It is also the attempt to discover one's true self. Most people fear the prodigious effort this requires and prefer to keep busy, as the frantic pace of the modern world requires, thereby hiding from themselves and suppressing the awareness that each of us is unique, has only one life to live and should not waste it on trivia. Yet the object of culture is to bring into existence true human beings who transcend our animal nature: these are philosophers, artists and saints. The first two enable nature to become self-aware; the saint, by suppressing his individuality, fulfils the ultimate purpose of nature, its 'redemption from itself' (*UM* 161). This surprisingly religious language reflects Schopenhauer's interest in Hinduism and Buddhism.

How can Schopenhauer serve as an educator? He is exemplary, in particular, because he did philosophy outside the universities. His brief business career, although he did not enjoy it, gave him some experience of non-academic work. And he himself was fortunate enough to have an educator, Goethe, whom he knew personally. Unlike the philosophers, Schopenhauer was free to pursue truth: '*The Schopenhauerian man voluntarily takes upon himself the suffering involved in being truthful*' (*UM* 152, emphasis in original). His example educates people not for but *against* the age they live in. Nietzsche quotes Emerson to underline that philosophy should not be comfortable but dangerous: when a new thinker arrives, says Emerson, it is as though a fire had broken out in a great city, putting everything in danger.

In this regard, Schopenhauer lived his philosophy, as Nietzsche insists a philosopher ought to do. 'I respect a philosopher just insofar as he can provide an example [. . .]. But the example must be given by his visible life, and not merely by books, as the philosophers of Greece taught by their expression, posture, clothing, food, habits, more than through speaking, let alone writing' (*UM* 136). Here Nietzsche seems to anticipate his own later lifestyle after resigning his university post, and also the attempts to lead an exemplary life, largely outside universities, by such twentieth-century philosophers as Ludwig Wittgenstein and Bertrand Russell.

In living his philosophy, not just writing it, Schopenhauer, in Nietzsche's view, joined hands with the earliest Greek philosophers. Mainly in early 1873 Nietzsche composed (but never published) a study of the pre-Socratics, or, as he prefers to call them, the pre-Platonic philosophers, known only from surviving fragments, who lived in the seventh and sixth centuries BCE, long before Plato (*c.* 427–348 BCE). The early Greeks steered a course between barbaric ignorance and excessive desire for knowledge, which, by separating learning from life, turns into another form of barbarism. With the Greeks, philosophy fed into life, and the philosopher had a prominent role in culture. Philosophy was not yet a recognized social role, let alone a job. The philosophers stood out because of their noble personal character, which was entirely consonant with the content of their thinking.

Among these philosophers, Nietzsche's favourite is clearly Heraclitus, who lived around 500 BCE. His predecessor Anaximander had divided reality into Being and Becoming, with the implication that Becoming, the ever-changing life that we experience, marks a fall from the static perfection of Being. Heraclitus denied that there was any such division. For him, the world originated from fire and was a continual flux of creation and destruction. There was no distinct Being. Reality consisted in action, inasmuch as to be real meant having an effect on other real things (Nietzsche's exposition benefits from the relation between the words *wirklich*, 'real', and *wirken*, 'to have an effect', and from quoting a similar argument from Schopenhauer). Hence there was incessant conflict, analogous to the conflict which was central to early Greek culture in the form of the *agon*.

This continual creation corresponds, in Nietzsche's interpretation, to art:

> A becoming and passing away, building and destroying, without any moral responsibility, in eternal, unchanging innocence, belongs in this world only to the play of the artist and the child. And just as the child and the artist plays, so the ever-living fire plays, builds and destroys, in innocence – and this is the game the Aeon plays with itself. (KSA I 830)

So reality is continual flux, morally neutral and with no purpose or meaning beyond the meaning the artist gives it. Nietzsche would remain deeply attached to this view, presupposing it, even where it is not explicit, throughout his later works.

3

The Aphorist

Nietzsche still had to earn his living as a professor of classical philology at the University of Basel. The work was hard: thirteen contact hours per week, plus the time needed to prepare his lectures and to mark his students' work. He was a conscientious and by all accounts successful teacher. In addition, he did his share of administration: in January 1874 he was appointed dean of the arts faculty, and later he features in documents as sub-dean. He felt frustrated that all this drudgery was preventing him from doing the original work he knew himself to be capable of, and compared himself to a horse yoked to the plough and unable to look to right or left (to mother and sister, 3 December 1874). In January 1875 he said that his profession had turned into 'curious misery':

> At present and for a couple of semesters I have so much to do, that I get from one day to the next in an absolute daze; that is what 'duty' requires and yet I often feel that in doing this 'duty' I am neglecting my real *duty*.
> (To Malwida von Meysenbug, 2 January 1871)

The demands of his job were made worse by the precarious state of his health. From about 1873 until his final breakdown in January 1889 Nietzsche's letters are full of harrowing descriptions of his sufferings. One example may suffice:

I have a *very bad* time behind me and perhaps a worse ahead of me. My stomach was out of control, even with an absurdly rigorous diet, headaches of the most violent kind lasting for several days and returning a few days later, hours of vomiting without having eaten anything, in short, the machine seemed about to disintegrate, and I won't deny that I sometimes wished it would. Great tiredness, difficulty walking along the street, intense sensitivity to light [. . .]. (To Gersdorff, 26 June 1875)

At times he suffered prolonged pain, lasting thirty hours at a stretch, which he ascribed to neuralgia. His eyesight became so bad that he had to hold a page close to his eyes in order to read it, and even then the letters seemed sometimes to form indistinguishable lumps. He carried a parasol to keep off strong sunlight. In 1877 he told his mother that he could use his eyes only for an hour and a half per day. In February 1876 he found himself too ill to lecture. For the academic year 1876–7 the university granted him leave of absence on health grounds (and although Nietzsche offered to give up his salary, the university continued paying it, subtracting only the cost of replacement teaching at the Pädagogium). He returned to his post in October 1877 and was relieved of his schoolteaching duties in March 1878, but in May 1879, aged 34, he felt compelled to offer his resignation. The university granted him a pension of 3,000 Swiss francs annually, which was enough for a single man to live on frugally. Thereafter Nietzsche, who also believed he was acutely sensitive to atmosphere, lived an itinerant life, seeking out congenial climates and alternating between the Mediterranean coast and the Swiss Alps.

The doctors Nietzsche consulted seem not to have been helpful. Hermann Immermann, the professor of pathology at Basel, who was in effect Nietzsche's GP, diagnosed a stomach ulcer. A German doctor whom Nietzsche called on in Naples in February 1877 spoke of neuralgia. Nietzsche seems not to have consulted an eye

Nietzsche, *c.* 1875, photograph by Friedrich Hermann Hartmann.

specialist until he wrote to the Basel ophthalmologist Dr Schiess in 1877. The various doctors looked only at particular symptoms without considering how they might be related. Nietzsche did rather better with Dr Otto Eiser, an unusually cultivated physician who was a friend of the Wagners and had read all Nietzsche's publications. They met in August 1877 in a remote part of Switzerland where the Eiser family were holidaying. Nietzsche developed such confidence in Eiser that the following month he travelled to Frankfurt for a consultation. Eiser was astonished that Nietzsche had had so little contact with his doctor in Basel and that the latter had not discussed his case with an ophthalmologist. He decided that severe retinal damage to Nietzsche's eyes had affected his brain and brought on the headaches and other symptoms, combined with cerebral overstrain through excessive mental activity. He recommended that Nietzsche should for the next few years refrain from reading, writing and immoderate mental or physical exertion, avoid strong light, follow a careful diet and not try to harden himself by wearing thin clothes, sitting in unheated rooms or taking long, strenuous walks. Whatever the value of his advice may have been, Dr Eiser was indiscreet enough to break patient confidentiality by writing about Nietzsche's case in great detail to the Wagners. Wagner replied with the crass opinion that Nietzsche's problems were due to excessive masturbation. When Nietzsche heard of this, he broke off contact with Eiser.

The story of Nietzsche's struggle against illness may be seen (as he wanted it to be seen) as a triumph of the will. He felt that his sufferings were the precondition for new intellectual insights. Hence he wrote to Eiser in January 1880: 'My existence is a *terrible burden*: I would long since have ended it, if I did not make the most instructive trials and experiments in the moral and intellectual sphere precisely in this state of suffering and almost absolute self-denial – this joyous quest for insight brings me to heights where I am victorious over all my torments and hopelessness. On the whole

I am happier than ever before in my life' – despite the afflictions which he proceeds to list.

So did Nietzsche in some sense welcome his sufferings? He was remarkably slow to consult doctors, and when he did, he ignored their advice. For example, although Eiser advised him to keep warm, Nietzsche's letters often report that he is sitting in an unheated room in winter because he can afford neither a portable stove nor a south-facing room. Granted, he had to be careful with money, but he might have given comfort and health a higher priority. To what extent was his lifestyle a demonstration of his strong will, as in the incident at school when he deliberately burnt his hand? Having made the will his central philosophical concept, was he living his philosophy, as he had praised Schopenhauer and the pre-Socratics for doing?

After resigning his professorship, Nietzsche became a homeless wanderer, living in rented rooms and making expensive and uncomfortable journeys (sometimes by sea, usually in trains with bare wooden seats) in search of a congenial climate. In the winters we find him at Genoa, Venice, the Italian lakes or the French Riviera. In the summer he usually went to the Swiss Alps, initially favouring St Moritz; but this was becoming a popular tourist resort and correspondingly expensive, so he moved further up the Engadin Valley to the village of Sils Maria, 1,800 metres above sea level, where the house he lived in is now a museum. Occasionally he thought of travelling further, to the North African resort of Biskra or to Oaxaca on the Mexican plateau, but these never became serious plans (letters to Heinrich Köselitz, 14 August 1881, 4 March 1882).

By this time, Nietzsche had discarded both his earlier idols, Wagner and Schopenhauer. His estrangement from Wagner was painful, gradual and never complete. It was bound up with what seemed the accomplishment of Wagner's lifelong endeavours, and of the hopes for Germany's future Nietzsche had expressed in

The Nietzsche Museum at Sils Maria.

The Birth of Tragedy: the opening of the Festival Theatre at Bayreuth as a home for Wagner's music-dramas and as the venue for the first performance of the four-part *Ring*. In April 1872 the Wagners left Tribschen for a house in Bayreuth. Nietzsche was saddened by his last visit to Tribschen: 'I spent a few days there as though amid mere ruins, melancholy days' (to Rohde, 30 April 1872). The following month he was present in Bayreuth for the ceremonial laying of the Festival Theatre's foundation stone.

The theatre opened in August 1876 with the premiere of the *Ring* on four successive evenings. It was a star-studded national occasion, attended by crowned heads and many titled and prominent figures. The Kaiser paid a brief visit; the Khedive of Egypt, the emperor of Brazil and of course Wagner's financial backers were present. Nietzsche later recalled his horror at the vulgar razzmatazz and the dominance of the most odious nationalism: '*What had happened?* – Wagner had been translated into German!' (*EH* '*HA*' 2). To make matters worse, the performances fell far short of expectations.

Wagner's theatrical vision outstripped the available technical resources. The rainbow bridge on which the gods are supposed to enter Asgard, the giants in *Das Rheingold*, the Valkyries on horseback, the cardboard dragon in *Siegfried*, all looked ridiculous. Nietzsche, unable to stand the philistine atmosphere, retreated to a nearby sanatorium, from which he wrote to his sister of his 'boundless disappointment' (6 August 1876).

From then on, Nietzsche's opinion of Wagner's music declined. In 1880 he described it as a reaction against the spirit of the Enlightenment, based on German national feeling (*HA* II 171). *Parsifal* (1882) struck him as a repellent homage to Christianity. In his polemic *The Case of Wagner* (1888), he described Wagner as decadent and neurotic, and concluded that his art was sick. Wagner was less a composer than a showman. And yet Nietzsche retained the warmest personal gratitude to Wagner. 'I would not lose the Tribschen days from my life for any price. Days of intimacy, serenity, sublime accidents – *profound* moments. I do not know how others got on with Wagner; but no clouds ever crossed our sky' (*EH* 'Clever' 5).

As for Schopenhauer, although some of his ideas play an essential role in *The Birth of Tragedy*, it is not clear that Nietzsche ever actually subscribed to Schopenhauer's philosophy. In his 'Untimely Meditation' on Schopenhauer, he praises the person as an exemplar of dedication to truth and to genuine, non-academic philosophy. By Nietzsche's own account, he turned definitively against Schopenhauer around 1876: 'About that time I grasped that my instinct went in the opposite direction to Schopenhauer's: towards a justification of life, even in its most terrible, ambiguous and mendacious forms' (autumn 1887, *KSA* XII 354–5). By 1877 he could express his firm conviction that Schopenhauer's metaphysics was false (to Carl Fuchs, 29 July 1877). Henceforth he would work out ideas antithetical to Schopenhauer's. Schopenhauer sought to escape from the Will, Nietzsche to affirm and strengthen it.

Franz von Lenbach, *Malwida von Meysenbug*, 1885, pastel.

Schopenhauer thought life not worth living; Nietzsche thought life infinitely worth living for those who were strong enough. Schopenhauer saw art as a temporary escape from the Will; Nietzsche saw art as an indispensable illusion which stimulated the will to live.[1]

Nietzsche was now moving into a new phase of his life. Fortunately he made some friends who could help him. One was Malwida von Meysenbug (1816–1903), a woman of strong character and liberal sympathies who especially championed women's education. Defying her conservative and aristocratic family, she had supported the revolutions of 1848, and to escape police harassment she moved in 1852 to London. There she worked as a governess to Olga and Natalie, the young daughters of the Russian revolutionary Alexander Herzen; to Olga she eventually became an adoptive mother. From 1862 she lived in Italy for health reasons. She met Nietzsche through her friends the Wagners, whose wedding she attended as a witness. To Nietzsche she was a maternal figure, as is clear from the warm letter he wrote her on 14 April 1876 after reading her three-volume autobiography, *Memoirs of an Idealist* (1875). In April 1876 Meysenbug suggested that Nietzsche should spend a year staying with her in Italy, and on 26 October he joined her in a hotel in Naples.

On the journey to Naples Nietzsche had two companions. One was Albert Brenner, a student of his from Basel, who was suffering from consumption and whom Meysenbug had taken under her wing. The other, an important figure in Nietzsche's intellectual and emotional life over the next few years, was Paul Rée (1849–1901). They had met in 1873 in Basel, where Rée was lecturing on philosophy. Rée, who came from a North German commercial family of Jewish descent, published two books, *Psychological Meditations* (1875), modelled on the French aphorists, and *The Origin of Moral Sentiments* (1877), owing much to British philosophers from Locke to Hume; Nietzsche read both with intense interest.

After meeting with Meysenbug, the whole party went to Sorrento on the Gulf of Naples, where Nietzsche, Rée and Brenner stayed in adjacent rooms in a hotel, the Villa Rubinacci. During the day they worked or walked, enjoying the climate and the views; in the evenings they formed a reading circle, and as both Nietzsche and Meysenbug suffered from eye trouble, Rée or Brenner read aloud. Their programme was ambitious. They began with Burckhardt's *History of Greek Culture* in the form of lecture notes written up by a student, then moved on to the Greek historians Thucydides and Herodotus. Next Rée took them through his favourite French writers (with some of whom Nietzsche had long been familiar): Montaigne, La Rochefoucauld, Vauvenargues, La Bruyère and Stendhal. They also read *Thought and Reality* by the Russian philosopher Afrikan Spir,[2] Ranke's *History of the Popes* and the New Testament. Their discussions must have been enriched by Rée's extensive knowledge of natural science, which he had studied in Berlin. This reading group, where ideas were presented, shared and discussed, was of crucial importance in fostering the new intellectual direction and the marked stylistic change that would now characterize Nietzsche's works, beginning with *Human, All-Too-Human*, which he was working on in Sorrento.

Another friendship, of much longer duration than the one with Rée, also dates from this period: with Heinrich Köselitz (1854–1918). Köselitz, a musician, so much admired *The Birth of Tragedy* that in 1875 he and a friend paid Nietzsche a visit, with a letter of introduction from Nietzsche's publisher Schmeitzner. This is the impression Nietzsche made:

> we were struck by his appearance. A military man, not a scholar! Although we had expected the author of the *Anti-Strauss* to be somewhat brusque, we were surprised by his kindness, his heartfelt seriousness, the absence of any sarcasm . . . The impression was one of exceptional self-control. Strict

with himself, strict in matters of principle, his judgements of people, on the other hand, were extremely benevolent.[3]

Nietzsche induced him to adopt the professional alias 'Peter Gast', on the grounds that nobody with a name like Köselitz could possibly make a musical career. From 1878 Köselitz lived mainly in Venice, where Nietzsche sometimes visited him. Köselitz performed selflessly the demanding task of caring for the invalid, and also transcribed his notes or took his dictation; much of *Human, All-Too-Human* was prepared for publication by Köselitz in this way. After Nietzsche's breakdown Köselitz would work for Elisabeth Nietzsche in transcribing selections from the notebooks as *The Will to Power*.

One reason Nietzsche valued his friend was that, with his failing eyesight, he needed people to read to him, as Rée had done in Sorrento. When he visited Köselitz in Venice, the latter read novels aloud to him: Adalbert Stifter's *Der Nachsommer* (1857) and Gottfried Keller's great Swiss Bildungsroman *Der grüne Heinrich* (Green Henry, second edition of 1880) – testimony to Nietzsche's fine literary taste. In Naumburg in November 1879 his mother read to him from Gogol, Lermontov, Edgar Allan Poe, Bret Harte and Mark Twain (to Overbeck, 14 November 1879); he was particularly taken by *The Adventures of Tom Sawyer*, and gave Overbeck a copy. His own book collection was a hindrance to his itinerant lifestyle: on 4 October 1884 he complains to his mother that his 104 kilograms of books are a 'club foot' that hampers his movements.

Nietzsche wanted to expand his one-sided classical education. 'The small amount of work I can do with my eyes', he wrote to Overbeck on 20/21 August 1881, 'is almost exclusively devoted to physiological and medical studies (I am so badly educated – and there is so much I must *know* properly!)'. This letter contains a list of specialized works on physics which he wanted Overbeck to procure for him. Nietzsche was a very active reader. He argued in letters and notebooks with state-of-the-art works on physics such as *The Mechanics of Heat* (1867) by Julius Robert Mayer, the physicist who in 1841 had formulated the first law of thermodynamics concerning the conservation of energy (see, for example, the letter to Köselitz of 20 April 1882). The importance for Nietzsche of his extensive reading in natural science has only recently been recognized.

If reading was difficult, so was writing. Nietzsche often worked out his thoughts while walking and then used short periods when his illness abated to write them up. He described to Köselitz how he had written *Human, All-Too-Human*: 'Everything, except for a few lines, was thought out *while walking* and sketched in pencil in 6 small notebooks: the *re*-writing almost always made me ill' (5 October 1879). Köselitz then made a fair copy for the printer and later helped Nietzsche to correct the proofs. In 1881 Nietzsche acquired a typewriter, hoping that he would soon learn to touch-type and thus spare his eyes, but the machine, though expensive, often broke down and had to be repaired (anticipating people's initial experiences with personal computers a century later). A number of typescript letters survive, but it is not clear how far the typewriter helped him to produce his books.

This working process helps to explain the character of Nietzsche's later books. While his previous works had been connected treatises, divided into sections (admittedly with considerable scope for digression), his books henceforth consist of many short numbered paragraphs, sometimes consisting of a single sentence, rarely as long as four pages. These can best be defined as extended aphorisms. His familiarity with the French aphorists may have made this form congenial, but his main reason for adopting it was ill health: since it was only for short periods that he could use his eyes and be free from disabling headaches, he was compelled to adopt what he called 'the accursed telegram style' (to Köselitz, 5 November 1879).

Human, All-Too-Human, written in Sorrento in 1876–7 and published in 1878 and 1880,[4] surprised Nietzsche's readers by turning decisively away from German themes and adopting a distinctively French literary and intellectual style. The first edition was dedicated to Voltaire, who had died just a century earlier, and after its publication Nietzsche reported receiving from an unknown correspondent in Paris a bust of Voltaire, with a note reading 'L'âme de Voltaire fait ses compliments à Frédéric Nietzsche' (letter to Köselitz, 31 May 1878). Like the works that followed, *Daybreak* (1881) and *The Gay Science* (1882), it reflects Nietzsche's enthusiastic reading of the French moralists with their sceptical psychological analyses. On the train journey to Sorrento he commended them to a fellow passenger, Isabella von Pahlen (later von Ungern-Sternberg), who had noticed him reading the *Maxims* of La Rochefoucauld: 'He praised the gift of the French, La Rochefoucauld, Vauvenargues, Condorcet, and especially Pascal, for pointed expression, which gave an idea the sharp relief of a medal.'[5] However, Nietzsche had marked preferences among these writers. Pascal was fascinating for the radicalism of his thought, which made him a stimulating intellectual antagonist: in denying that life without religious belief could be meaningful or sustainable, Pascal anticipated the pessimism of Schopenhauer.[6] According to Ida Overbeck, wife of his former colleague Franz, Nietzsche counted himself among the 'aristocratic moralists' and particularly liked La Rochefoucauld, but disapproved of Chamfort for associating with men of the French Revolution.[7]

It will be convenient here to discuss *Human, All-Too-Human*, *Daybreak* and *The Gay Science* together, with occasional glances forward to the development of their themes in *Beyond Good and Evil* (1886) and other late writings.[8] Nietzsche begins by analysing and questioning the assumptions of modern civilization and gradually moves towards sketching a new set of values, which will find vigorous expression in the prophecies of *Zarathustra* and the discursive texts of his last period.

Enlightenment

Early in *Human, All-Too-Human* Nietzsche announces his mission to sustain the Enlightenment. On its banner are inscribed three names: Petrarch, Erasmus and Voltaire (*HA* 26). Petrarch is mentioned because of his share in the rediscovery of classical literature; Erasmus as the great textual critic of the Bible, with his edition of the Greek New Testament; and Voltaire as the witty campaigner against oppression and obscurantism by the Church.[9]

Nietzsche charges Germany with rejecting the Enlightenment. By exalting emotion over reason, it became the centre of Romanticism. Romantic scholarship studied the traditions of the past that survived in popular culture and in legal and political customs. Thereby, however, it ultimately frustrated its own aims. It provided the enlightened enquirer with tools to reveal the historical origins, and thus undermine the authority, of the very traditions which it sought to defend against the Enlightenment. 'It is this Enlightenment', says Nietzsche, 'that we now have to continue' (*D* 197).

The instrument of Nietzschean enlightenment is *Wissenschaft*. This word comprehends both natural science and humanist scholarship, including the philological study of texts in which Nietzsche was trained. It will be rendered here as 'science', but the reader is urged to remember that it implies rigorous intellectual enquiry into history and literature as well as nature and medicine. Even in a very late work, *The Antichrist*, Nietzsche advocates 'the two great opponents of all superstition: philology and medicine' (*A* 47).

Science, in this extended sense, and thus enlightenment, originated with the Greeks. The Greeks excelled in an unembarrassed, realistic apprehension of the world. It was this sense of the real that enabled them to become 'natural scientists, historians, geographers and philosophers' (*VMS* 220). They were able to perceive the typical in every phenomenon and thus arrive, with the aid of reason, at plausible generalizations: Nietzsche illustrates this gift particularly from the first great historian, Thucydides (*D* 168). Hence they 'created science' (*VMS* 221). This view of the Greeks remains intact in 1888: Nietzsche praises their '*sense of fact, the last and most valuable of all senses*' (*A* 59).

Besides *Wissenschaft*, another key word is *Erkenntnis*. Although it will be lamely translated here as 'knowledge', it implies, more than any English term, an active, energetic search for knowledge, and a process of discovery which can give intense satisfaction (*D* 98). The satisfaction it gave Nietzsche is attested by the moving letter to Dr Eiser in which, having described his sufferings, he says he would already have thrown off the burden of life were it not for the 'joyous thirst for knowledge' that sustains him (early January 1880). The passion for knowledge, Nietzsche tells us, is a modern discovery: to the ancients, virtue was more important than knowledge (*GS* 123).

The search for knowledge requires honesty (*Redlichkeit*). This is about the only moral concept that Nietzsche does not dismantle, although in his later work he repeatedly asks why we want it. It is a post-Christian virtue (*D* 456), connected with scholarly rigour, and with the 'intellectual conscience' that most people still lack (*GS* 2, 335). The commitment to intellectual rigour creates a clear, bright, bracing, male atmosphere, which frightens the uninitiated; once one is accustomed to it, however, it is the only air one would want to breathe (*GS* 293).

Enlightenment and religion are incompatible. It is clear to Nietzsche that nobody with an intellectual conscience can accept religion (*HA* 109), least of all Christianity, which is a strange, incongruous survival from the ancient world:

A god who sires children with a mortal woman; a wise man who tells people no longer to work or to judge, but to attend to the signs that the end of the world is at hand; a justice that accepts the innocent person as vicarious sacrifice; someone who orders his disciples to drink his blood; prayers for miraculous interventions; sins committed against a god, atoned for by a god; fear of a Beyond to which death is the gateway; the shape of the cross as symbol amid an age that no longer knows the purpose and the disgrace of the cross – how hideously all this breathes upon us, as through from the grave of the ancient past! Can one believe that such a thing is still believed? (*HA* 113)[10]

In fact, according to Nietzsche, such Christianity is scarcely believed any longer. Truly active people in the present day have discarded Christianity, at least inwardly, while more contemplative people have reduced Christianity to a vague optimism and an attitude, in the face of life's undeniable evils, of low expectations and resignation. In this diluted version of Christianity, 'God, freedom and immortality' have been replaced with a nebulous belief in benevolence and decency, which are supposed to prevail in the cosmos. This is 'the euthanasia of Christianity' (*D* 92). Nietzsche wishes that the many people in Europe who no longer believe in God – he estimates their number at 20 million – would make themselves known to one another and join forces to form a new power transcending divisions of nation and class (*D* 96).

Nietzsche follows a long-standing idea, formulated by the Roman poet Lucretius and espoused in the Enlightenment especially by David Hume, that religion originated from fear.[11] Primitive humans projected their own feelings onto inanimate objects and supposed that the latter could be controlled and propitiated by religious ceremonies, including sacrifices.[12] At a later stage, that of classical antiquity, a variety of gods were imagined as residing in a remote space and occasionally visiting mortals. Polytheism, according to Nietzsche, had distinct advantages. It gave scope for the imagination by letting people invent a variety of gods and other supernatural or semi-divine beings, whereas monotheism confines people to a 'standard God' and hence imposes a single standard model of humanity (*GS* 143).

By imagining their gods with human passions and faults, the Greeks were better able to accept their own nature and even to celebrate their own 'all-too-human' failings (*vms* 220). They understood crime, as in the myths of Prometheus and Oedipus, but had no conception of sin (*gs* 135; cf. *bt* 9).

Judaism and Christianity brought sin into the world (*ha* 124, *ws* 78). They required humanity to compare itself to a perfect and all-powerful God. By this measure, humanity was bound to fall miserably short. This resulting feeling of self-reproach generated the need for redemption and salvation. People were taught to hate themselves: Nietzsche refers to Pascal's famous statement 'the self is hateful' (*d* 63, *vms* 385),[13] and describes St Paul as 'the Jewish Pascal' (*d* 68). They were made to despise nature, the body and sex. By condemning the bodily sensations that everyone has by nature, Christianity ensured that everybody would be miserable (*d* 76). Ascetics who mortified the flesh by starvation and self-torment were held up for admiration. Throughout the Middle Ages, the highest human achievement was considered to be mystical visions – experiences which in the light of modern medicine can be attributed to psychological disturbance (*ma* 126, *d* 66). Although we nowadays deplore physical torture, we still underestimate the mental torture that Christianity imposed on millions of believers by terrifying them with the prospect of hell (*d* 77).[14]

All this is a powerful indictment. But around 1880 Nietzsche's view of Christianity is more differentiated than it will become later in the decade. He describes how, in the decadent Roman society evoked by the satirist Juvenal, the quiet unworldliness of early Christians and their exaltation of the soul must have been refreshing, like a remnant of the 'good antiquity' embodied in Greek philosophers (*vms* 224). And in more recent times, in the classical French culture which Nietzsche so values, he finds a series of refined, intellectually subtle Christians whom he cannot help admiring: from Pascal, 'in his union of fire, wit and

honesty the first of all Christians', down to the intellectually and
morally stringent Jansenists of Port-Royal. Without the Counter-
Reformation, and its Protestant counterpart Pietism, which sought
to deepen the spiritual experience of believers, we would never have
had the spiritually profound music of Palestrina and Bach (*HA* 219).

What Can I Know?

Although enlightened science and scholarship have disproved the
claims of religion, it is much harder to shake off the authority of
metaphysics. This term covers all doctrines claiming that there
is another, permanent reality behind the ever-changing world
perceived by the senses; that this other reality can be apprehended
intellectually or spiritually; and that it is somehow more real than
the world we know through our senses. Christian belief in the
unchanging divine realm is one such doctrine; another is Plato's
theory of Forms or Ideas, of which earthly things are merely a copy;
yet another is Kant's *Ding an sich*, the reality that we can never
access because our minds are so constructed as to experience the
world only in terms of time and space.

   Nietzsche aims to undercut metaphysical beliefs in a permanent
other reality by investigating how such beliefs originated.
Reality may well be in continual flux (*HA* 16, recalling Nietzsche's
admiration for the pre-Socratic philosopher Heraclitus, who
held this view). It can therefore never provide a basis for belief in
something permanent. There is really no such thing as a 'thing'
(*HA* 19). Nietzsche rejects materialism: rather than classical
atomism, which held that the basic constituents of reality were
infinitesimal bits of solid matter, he prefers the theory by the Jesuit
physicist Ruggero Boscovich (1711–1787) that 'atoms' are complexes
of energy (see *BGE* 12). Even the supposed laws of mathematics
and logic are traced back to intellectual errors. No two objects in
experience are really identical. Hence the concept of number is

based on an error – the supposition that two merely similar phenomena are identical and can therefore be counted (*HA* 19). But it is an error with survival value. A primeval creature searching for food found something similar to its previous meal and devoured it without stopping to see if it was actually the same; another creature that paused to reflect and compare would have starved (*GS* 111). Similarly, most of our supposed knowledge about the world consists of life-sustaining errors (*GS* 110; one might nowadays prefer to say 'fictions', but Nietzsche uses the more provocative term). The urge to find truth comes at a very late stage in human development, and it often reveals to us how little we know or can know. For example, we now know that the concept of 'cause' does not *explain* the relation between two successive events; it just says, 'whenever A happens, B happens,' but we are none the wiser as to why (*GS* 112).[15]

Does this mean that all our supposed knowledge is based on falsehood, and truth is inaccessible or even non-existent? Sometimes Nietzsche does say this, notably in an essay of 1873 which has received much attention in recent decades, although as he himself did not publish it, its place in the Nietzsche canon is questionable: 'On Truth and Lie [*sic*] in an Extra-Moral Sense'. Here again, the intellect is not a means of disinterested enquiry, but a survival mechanism. It uses deceit just as animals use protective colouring. In order to escape from constant warfare and to live peaceably together, people share a language that expresses a set of agreed truths. But the words composing language are simply nervous stimuli, translated into images and thence into sounds. When words are used to express general ideas and concepts, they are still further removed from any original experience. Language can never correspond to 'the essence of things'; the truth it purports to express is merely 'a mobile army of metaphors'. Even mathematics is based only on metaphors of time and space. Nothing in language, nor in our experience, is 'true in itself'; the 'essence of things' never appears in the empirical world.

This has often been taken as a devastating argument against the possibility of truth.[16] However, it argues only that language and experience do not give access to the 'essence of things'. Here 'truth' is conceived as existing in some transcendent realm – another example, in fact, of the metaphysical illusions that Nietzsche denounces. In the same essay, however, he rejects this claim, asserting that there is *no* transcendent or absolute truth. It makes no sense to ask whether an insect or a bird perceives the world more or less correctly than we do, because there is no standard of correct perception, hence no absolutely true knowledge of the world. But this contradicts the rest of the essay. If 'truth' is not just unavailable, but inconceivable, then it makes no sense to proclaim that our knowledge is false.[17] Rather, as Nietzsche says elsewhere, we have cobbled together a world in which we can live; if its basic components (cause and effect, motion and rest and so on) cannot be proved, but must be taken as articles of faith, that does not matter, for life is not an argument (*GS* 121). The concept of truth makes perfect sense within the rules of the game – the standards of rational acceptability – imposed by our sensory and intellectual apparatus. We just need to remember that assertions about the world can never claim absolute truth, but only varying degrees of probability (*VMS* 7); the tree of knowledge produces 'probability, but not truth' (*WS* 1). Here Nietzsche is formulating the now recognized principle of scientific and scholarly research, that a conclusion can be established beyond reasonable doubt, but never with absolute certainty, and is always in principle open to correction. Accordingly, Nietzsche talks constantly of the search for truth. He unmasks the errors of religious and philosophical thinkers in order to replace them with the truth, or (what amounts to the same thing) with explanations that are very much more probable.

If metaphysics is illusory, humanity has no contact with any 'higher world'. It follows that humanity is part of nature and needs to be studied as such, while our understanding of nature itself needs to be freed from lingering metaphysical notions. Since nature is in flux, the concept of indestructible underlying matter is as false as the associated philosophical concept of substance. Nor is nature governed by laws: 'laws of nature' are merely an anthropomorphic metaphor for necessities. Even the regularities that the term denotes may apply merely in our small corner of the universe: 'the character of the world as a whole is chaos in all eternity' (GS 109). There is no purpose in nature; *a fortiori*, there is no purpose or plan in the existence of humanity. These theses, clearly formulated in 1882, will be explored further and asserted yet more forcefully later in the decade.

As part of nature, humanity is subject to the same necessities as all other natural beings, including evolution. Naturalists in Nietzsche's Germany had long accepted that nature was not a timeless order but was caught up in processes of change. Before Darwin, the most widely accepted theory of change in organic beings was that of Jean-Baptiste Lamarck (1744–1829), who argued that an organism changes in order to satisfy its needs in a challenging environment (thus giraffes gradually developed longer necks in order to reach the leaves of tall trees). After initial hesitation, German scientists accepted Darwin's theory of evolution as superior to Lamarck's. According to a notebook entry, Nietzsche accepted Darwinism by the early 1870s (KSA VII 461). He notes that although the idea of descent from apes offends people's pride, some past cultures thought it honourable to be descended fron animals or trees (D 31). But he did not agree with every feature of Darwinism. He accepted the idea of the struggle for existence, and even followed the biologist Wilhelm Roux (1850–1924) in conjecturing that such a struggle went on not only between organisms but within an organism: organs, cells and even molecules were in constant competition.[18] Such a struggle, however, had no purpose. Darwin's principle of utility, which maintains that variations are selected for their survival value, struck Nietzsche as too reminiscent of the principle of teleology, which had been banished from natural science.[19] Humanity, in his view, can no longer boast either of its origins, which lead back only to a grinning ape, or of its destiny, for it is not heading for a higher form of existence any more than ants or earwigs are (*D* 49). Evolution need not be progressive: it may lead to regress and degeneration. Humanity's development may run from ape to man and back again, in a biological decline comparable to the cultural decline caused by Christianity (*HA* 247).

'Purpose' is just one of the many concepts that we project onto the world. 'Chance' is another such concept: it only makes sense by contrast with 'purpose'. It is equally illegitimate to represent the cosmos as an organism or as a machine, or to apply the concepts of matter and substance. All these concepts we impose on nature are simply after-echoes of the obsolete belief in God (*GS* 109). We need to discard them, along with the idea that humanity is anything more than a natural being. We will then see nature as it is, freed from divinity, and ourselves as natural beings, together with 'pure, newly discovered, newly redeemed nature' (*GS* 109). Nietzsche retains the cleansing, transfiguring associations of the word 'redeemed' while rejecting its Christian overtones: we are to be redeemed *from* Christianity and *into* nature.

The Analysis of Morals

Turning to the observation of human life, Nietzsche presents himself as a moralist, which is quite different from being a preacher of morality (*WS* 19). He is an analyst of human behaviour, in the spirit of the great French moralists. He especially admired La Rochefoucauld for his pithy, polished formulations and for his insight in revealing the true motives underlying people's actions, as in the aphorism that Nietzsche quotes: 'What the world calls virtue is commonly nothing but a phantom formed by our passions to which a respectable name is given so that one can do what one wants with impunity' (*HA* 36). Nietzsche insists, however, that moralists are not to be confused with mean-minded people who seek to debunk the virtues they cannot appreciate. Rather, moralists reveal the complex motives behind the apparent simplicity of people's actions and skilfully unravel the self-deceptions in which people indulge (*WS* 20).

Analysing morality, Nietzsche emphasizes that moral beliefs are not considered judgements, but inherited prejudices. This is necessarily so: any society, if it is to last, must rely on shared principles which are taken for granted and beyond discussion, and assume the authority of tradition (*HA* 224). Nietzsche increasingly refers to this state of affairs by the shorthand *Sittlichkeit der Sitte*, 'morality of custom', conveying that custom (*Sitte*) is the real basis of morality (*Sittlichkeit*) (*D* 9).

Nietzsche picks up another Enlightenment theme by pointing out the diversity of morals in different countries and at different periods. To Hume, for example, the morality of ancient Greece, which set a high value on male–male love, and that of modern France, with its tolerance for adultery, differed so widely from that of Britain as to make it doubtful whether any single standard of morality could be set up.[20] Nietzsche, accepting that there are diverse moralities in the world, distinguishes them according to the 'rank order' (*Rangordnung*) they assign to various goods (*HA* 42). In present-day Europe, for example, it is considered immoral to prefer sensual indulgence to health, or well-being to freedom. But supposing an injured person, rather than relying on the legal system for redress, prefers to take personal revenge? We consider that immoral, but earlier cultures thought it moral to pursue blood-feuds. 'Immoral' conduct thus often means adhering to an earlier, less subtle and refined code of morality.

An increasingly prominent theme in Nietzsche's moral reflections is that of power. Early in *Human, All-Too-Human* he traces the origin of 'good' and 'evil' to the relations between a powerful ruling caste and a powerless mass of slaves, anticipating the famous distinction between master morality and slave morality that will be fully developed in the first treatise of *The Genealogy of Morals*. 'Good' implies power – above all, the power to retaliate an injury. For powerful people, the 'bad' are the weak, contemptible slaves who dare not retaliate. To the slaves, however, their oppressors are not just bad but evil, and for the powerless all power is stigmatized as wicked (*HA* 45; cf. *D* 189).

Reflecting further, Nietzsche transfers his emphasis from power over other people to the subjective sense of power (*Machtgefühl*), which he describes as the first effect of happiness (*D* 356). The Greeks valued this feeling highly; to them, power was important primarily as well-being, rather than serving useful purposes or enhancing one's reputation (*D* 360). In Christian Europe, the feeling of power came from having strong religious convictions. Nowadays it comes from having money: 'the means of satisfying power-hunger have changed, but the same volcano is still glowing' (*D* 204). In a modern democracy, the public enjoys a vicarious sense of power by supporting the actions of a powerful state (*D* 189). Power confers more happiness than anything else: 'Not necessity, not desire – no, the love of power is the demon of humanity' (*D* 262).

The sense of power needs to be enjoyed and discharged in action. Hence it underlies much of the behaviour discussed by moralists. Malice and cruelty are motivated not by the desire to hurt others, but by the desire to enjoy our own power. A child who hurts animals does not realize that they are different from toys (*HA* 104); a tyrant such as Xerxes was too remote from his subjects to imagine what they were suffering (*HA* 81). This benign interpretation of motives is rare in Nietzsche, however: a few pages earlier he describes how the weak use their power to hurt by causing distress to those who feel sorry for them, and rounds off this aphorism with a quotation from the French Romantic Prosper Mérimée: 'Sachez aussi qu'il n'y a rien de plus commun que de faire le mal pour le plaisir de le faire' (Know too that there is nothing commoner than doing harm for the pleasure of doing it; *HA* 50).[21]

Later Nietzsche describes the essential place of cruelty in the development of religion. A small community, governed by strict morality, will find pleasure and virtue in the enjoyment of ingenious cruelty. The gods are imagined as taking pleasure in the sufferings of humanity, and presently humans come to feel that they should accept and even seek suffering as a tribute to the gods or God (*D* 18). Thus Nietzsche outlines a theory of religion as sado-masochism: the divinity imposes suffering, the worshipper finds fulfilment in welcoming it.[22] Cruelty, Nietzsche says here, provides the most delicious feeling of power. He thus anticipates one of the bleakest assertions in *The Genealogy of Morals*: 'Watching suffering feels good, causing suffering even better' (*GM* II 6).

One might think that an urge to increase one's own sense of power by tormenting others would be counteracted by a feeling of compassion. Compassion, however, is subjected to the same remorseless analysis. Like malice, it is motivated primarily by the desire to enjoy one's own sense of power, which can be satisfied by helping the powerless as well as by torturing them (*HA* 103). The very word, which, like its German counterpart, *Mitleid*, means 'suffering with', is misleading. There is a great gulf between your toothache and my sympathy with your toothache. Even if I do feel pain on your behalf, my compassionate action is motivated by a desire to free myself from my own pain, and thus by egoism (*D* 133). Insofar as it causes vicarious pain, compassion does us harm (*D* 134). One should not criticize the stoical type of person who lacks compassion: he does not complain of his own sufferings, so lacks patience with others' complaints; he does not like feeling stirred by sympathy, because it threatens his manhood and his courage. This is egoistic, but so is compassion (*D* 133). Even when someone we love is suffering and we help them, we enjoy receiving their gratitude (*D* 138). Nietzsche refers approvingly to La Rochefoucauld's critique of sympathy as something which rational people should avoid.[23] All this amounts to an analysis of compassion which may be repellent, but is more subtle and differentiated than the tirades against compassion for which Nietzsche's later writings are notorious.

These analyses of particular moral concepts are framed within a general approach to questions of morality. Here Nietzsche admits his debt to the book *The Origin of the Moral Sentiments* by his friend Paul Rée, praised as 'one of the boldest and most cool-headed thinkers' (*HA* 37).[24] Rée, like Nietzsche, examines morals historically in the light of evolutionary theory. Primitive man valued those actions that were useful to the community, and called them 'good'; later the label 'good' survived after the reason for giving it was forgotten.[25] No action is really good or bad in itself.

Rée maintains that people are governed by egoistic impulses. Freedom of the will is an illusion: Rée cites a long list of philosophers, from Hobbes to Schopenhauer, in support of this claim. All events, including thoughts and sensations, in both animals and humans, result from prior causes. Every act of the will is necessary. It is therefore a mistake to assume that people are responsible for their actions, to blame them or to punish them. Punishment may serve for deterrence, by frightening others into refraining from anti-social behaviour, but it is futile as retribution, because the criminal could not have acted in any other way than he did.

Nietzsche in 1878 accepts these arguments with enthusiasm. He professes a strong, or, as William James called it, 'hard' determinism, insisting that all things happen by necessity.[26] A waterfall may seem to show us random movement, but an omniscient mind could calculate all its motion mathematically and prove its necessity (*HA* 106 – an unfortunate example, since at present chaos theory maintains that the movement of water is among the phenomena that cannot be predicted). The human will is not free. He insists that this determinism is not fatalism, because 'Turkish fatalism' assumes that fate is something alien to which humanity must blindly submit; but in fact each person *is* his own fate, and fulfils it whatever he does (*ws* 61). However, this seems to be a distinction, not between two kinds of determinism, but between two attitudes to determinism: passive acceptance and positive affirmation. It is perhaps an attempt to address the obvious problem posed by deterministic theories: although from the outside I may be a passive object of deterministic causation, from the inside I feel that I am constantly taking large and small decisions and acting on them, and there is no obvious way of reconciling these two perspectives. Determinism creates difficulties for the concept of the will, which becomes increasingly prominent in Nietzsche's thinking, and we shall see in a later chapter how he tries to cope with these difficulties.

From Nietzsche's hard determinism it follows that blame and responsibility are illusory. That being so, capital punishment feels worse than murder, because the murderer is the victim of his own upbringing and other circumstances, and he is being used merely as an instrument to deter others from murder (*HA* 70). We should instead treat criminals like mentally ill patients, with kindness and intelligence, providing them with a change of air, society and occupation, and discouraging them from futile self-torment through remorse; incorrigible criminals who hate themselves should be enabled to commit suicide (*D* 202).

More generally, once we have understood that the will is unfree, we will be able to discard any sense of guilt or sin. This at last will liberate us from the misery that Christianity has inflicted on humanity. The road will be open to a confident self-affirmation and an enjoyment of earthly pleasures such as the Greeks had. Self-affirmation will be based on a feeling of well-being; there will be nothing moral about it. Good will vanish as well as evil. Both concepts exist only in an imaginary metaphysical realm. In real life, apparent good is constantly changing into apparent evil, and vice versa, and science can explain this process by a 'chemistry of concepts and sensations' that dissolves all seeming antitheses (*HA* 1). 'Good actions are sublimated evil ones; evil actions are crude, stupid good ones' (*HA* 107). Thus Nietzsche opens up a perspective that is 'beyond good and evil'.

State and Society

Nietzsche, especially in the section of *Human, All-Too-Human* entitled 'A Glance at the State', casts a cold eye on modern European politics and society – reluctantly, for he considers politics unworthy of attention from intellectually gifted people (*D* 179). He sees that ideals of democracy and equality now have the upper hand. Subordination to authority is dying out (*HA* 441). Politicians are obliged to be demagogues (*HA* 438). A leader needs to impress the masses by the (real or apparent) strength of his will; if he can do that, he can have all the base qualities characteristic of the masses – violence, envy, conceit and so forth (*HA* 460). The masses have no ideal higher than comfort. The humanitarianism that is constantly preached rests on the idea of compassion, which Nietzsche has already shown to be hypocritical (*GS* 339).

Under the pretence of democracy, modern industrial society has reinvented slavery. Indeed, modern wage-slaves lead harder, less secure lives than slaves in traditional slave societies (*HA* 457). The cult of incessant hard work, which has spread from America to Europe, means that employers are also slaves, obliged constantly to keep their eye on the clock (*GS* 329). 'Anyone who does not have two-thirds of a day for himself is a slave, be he who he may: statesman, businessman, civil servant or academic' (*HA* 283). Earlier cultures valued leisure (*otium*, *HA* 284); nowadays, one has to apologize even for going on holiday, claiming that one's health demands it (*GS* 329). And yet this frantic work has no purpose and gives no pleasure. Most people work only for wages, hardly anyone because they really enjoy the work (GS 42). People cannot explain why they are wearing themselves out; they are in the grip of a social mechanism (HA 283). Hard work merely encourages dependence on alcohol, which Nietzsche declares to be Europe's poison (GS 42), along with Europe's other favourite narcotic, Christianity. Alcohol and Christianity are now being exported to the rest of the world and are hastening the extinction of uncivilized races overseas (GS 147).

Among the nineteenth-century critics of democracy, such as Alexis de Tocqueville, Thomas Carlyle and his own colleague Jacob Burckhardt, Nietzsche is perhaps the harshest. Like them, he finds it difficult to propose a realistic solution.[27] The answer is certainly not socialism, whether revolutionary or otherwise. Nietzsche dismisses as an absurd fantasy the idea that the overthrow of the present social order would introduce a better one. The futility of revolution has been demonstrated by the French Revolution, which, inspired by 'Rousseau's impassioned follies and half-lies', 'has dispelled the spirit of the Enlightenment and progressive development for a long time to come' (HA 463). Nietzsche much prefers the gradualism advocated by Voltaire; in reply to revolutionary optimism he adopts the slogan 'Écrasez l'infâme!' (Smash the vile thing!), which was Voltaire's battle-cry against the Catholic Church. Nietzsche is convinced that socialists just want power (HA 446) and the satisfaction of greed (HA 451). If they attained power, they would create a new despotism which would be worse than the despotisms of the past, because it would seek to eradicate the individual (HA 473). Discontented workers, rather than follow the 'Socialist Pied Pipers', should emigrate to Europe's expanding overseas colonies. Europe may then replace them by importing large numbers of docile Chinese labourers (D 206 – as was in fact done on the Pacific seaboard of the United States).

Not only socialism, but nationalism, represents a danger to Europe. Nationalism is at present being artificially encouraged, especially in Germany (as an ideological foundation for the Reich established in 1871). However, it is bound eventually to be counteracted by developments (which social theorists nowadays would label 'modernity') that Nietzsche sums up as follows:

> Trade and industry, communication by books and letter, the shared character of all higher culture, the rapidity with which people change their dwellings and surroundings, the nomadic life led at present by everyone except landowners – these circumstances must necessarily weaken and in the end annihilate nations, at least those of Europe: so that from them all, thanks to continual interbreeding, there must emerge a mixed race, that of European man. (*HA* 475)

This mixed race should have a large Jewish component. Not only have the Jews produced Christ, Spinoza and the Bible, but during the darkness of the Middle Ages they held on to 'the banner of enlightenment' and helped to ensure the emergence of a rational and non-mythic understanding of the world. 'If Christianity did everything to Orientalize the Occident, Judaism has helped repeatedly to Occidentalize it again: which in a certain sense means making Europe's mission and history into a continuation of those of Greece' (*HA* 475).

When Nietzsche commends 'good Europeans', he is not talking about international sympathies; he means people to whom their European identity is more important than their nationality, and who are helping to create a post-national European elite. These good Europeans are akin to the 'free spirits' whom Nietzsche also praises. Their mission is to promote good writing and to prepare for the distant day when good Europeans will assume the task of 'leading and supervising the culture of the whole earth' (*ws* 87).

Might a future Europe pick up the threads of enlightened, elitist antiquity that were severed by Christianity? Glancing back to the Greeks, Nietzsche sees hope, not in Athenian democracy, but in the tyrants or autocrats who emerged in many Greek states. Their rise is usually attributed to the corruption of democracy. But if so, corruption is welcome, for these tyrants were the first individuals and thus the ancestors of figures like Julius Caesar and, most recently, Napoleon (*GS* 23). Nietzsche does not have a social blueprint for Europe's future. He notes, however, that socialism is encouraged by the contempt that industrial workers feel for the faceless nonentities who employ them. Soldiers, on the other hand, feel respect and admiration for their commanders. Workers would obey readily if they felt their employers were entitled to rule them by superior birth (*GS* 40).

Here Nietzsche introduces the word *vornehm*, meaning 'aristocratic' or 'noble', but with reference more to manners than to birth. It will henceforth be rendered here as 'noble'. Nobility results from generations of training. It shows itself in bodily comportment: the noble person does not lounge in a chair but sits bolt upright (*D* 201). He shows his spiritual superiority by remaining pleasant and polite even in difficult situations. His evident power over himself enables him to exercise power over others. Nietzsche associates *Vornehmheit* especially with the aristocratic culture of seventeenth-century France. He also finds it among the Greeks, in a more pronounced form, because the Greek ruling elite constantly had before their eyes the contrast with a slave class, who did the manual work that the Greeks considered contemptible (*GS* 18).

Some degree of nobility, however, is possible also for the type of person Nietzsche describes as a free spirit. Such people have confidence in themselves, know that they will never do anything contemptible, and do not condemn any natural impulse as wicked (*GS* 294). They have overcome all conventional prejudices. They follow intellectual enquiry (*Erkenntnis*) wherever it leads them. They are content to live modestly and remain unknown to the great world. Their style of living and thinking reveals a 'refined heroism' (*HA* 291). The free spirit welcomes sunlight (the light of knowledge): 'Wherever we may come, it will always be free and sunny around us' (*HA* 291). Alas, as Nietzsche admits in the preface to *Human, All-Too-Human* he wrote in 1886, the 'free spirit' is as yet only an ideal. When writing *Human, All-Too-Human*, he was bitterly conscious of his isolation, and surrounded himself with such imaginary friends (*HA* preface 2).

In this preface, however, Nietzsche affirms that free spirits will appear in the future. He sketches their psychology, assuming that they are 'people of a lofty elite' (*HA* preface 3). Such people initially show their superior nature by their attachment to traditions, which inspire them with awe and a sense of obligation. To tear oneself free from the bonds of tradition involves a sudden shock, a violent urge for freedom. The free spirit must suffer years of loneliness, but he will gradually regain his health, and, in keeping with his dutiful nature, accept a new task, imposed on him by the future: that of determining the higher and lower values that should guide human life. Both the free spirit and the aristocrat will come into their own only in the future. And so Nietzsche's next books, beginning with the prophetic *Zarathustra*, are orientated towards the future.

4

The Prophet

Nietzsche was solitary by nature. But solitary people can also feel lonely. He told his motherly friend Malwida von Meysenbug that although he was richly blessed with friends, he also needed 'a good wife' (25 October 1874). Increasingly, as his health declined, he wanted such a person also to be his nurse and secretary.

Visiting Geneva in April 1876, Nietzsche met the conductor Hugo von Senger, whom he had known for some years, and two sisters from Riga (then in the Russian Empire) who were studying music with Senger. One of these, the 23-year-old Mathilde Trampedach, immediately attracted Nietzsche. After meeting her only three times, he wrote to her asking her to be his wife (11 April 1876), requesting an answer before his train left Geneva the following morning. He could not know that Trampedach was secretly in love with Senger, whom she would marry in 1879. She replied, naturally, with a tactful refusal, and Nietzsche appears to have had no hard feelings. With the help of Meysenbug, who liked match-making, he went on considering possible candidates, among them Meysenbug's ex-pupil Natalie Herzen; she, however, flatly refused. One wonders how serious such plans were, since Nietzsche also wrote that he could contemplate only a two-year marriage (to Rée, 21 March 1882).

Then, in 1882, Nietzsche met someone (as it happened, also from Russia) who completely overwhelmed his emotions. Louise von Salomé (1861–1937), always known as Lou, was the daughter of a general in the Russian Imperial service.[1] Brought up to speak German and French (the language of her father's Huguenot ancestors) much better than Russian, she was a highly intelligent, introspective, studious and independent-minded young woman who had discarded Christian belief in her teens. In 1879–80 she spent a year in Zurich with her mother as chaperone, attending university lectures on philosophy and the history of religion. Her health broke down, and early in 1882 her mother took her to Italy. Through a mutual friend she got to know Meysenbug, who, having a lifelong commitment to women's education, had assembled a circle of intelligent young women. On 17 March 1882 Paul Rée came to lecture to the group. Lou was immediately struck by him, and they became close friends. Rée urged Nietzsche, who was travelling in Italy, to come to Rome and meet the fascinating 'Russian woman'.

Nietzsche arrived in Rome late in April 1882. Lou in her memoirs recalls their first meeting, emphasizing Nietzsche's ceremonious manner:

> I recall this ceremoniousness even from our very first meeting, which took place in St Peter's, where Paul Rée, in a confessional box with a particularly good light, was ardently and piously occupied with his work notes, and to which Nietzsche had therefore been directed. He first greeted me with the words: 'From what stars have we fallen to meet each other here?'[2]

Nietzsche believed he had found in her a soulmate, linked to him by their fierce, unconventional intelligence and by their experience of illness. Her poem 'To Pain' moved him to tears: 'it sounds like a voice for which I have been waiting and waiting since my childhood' (to Köselitz, 13 July 1882). He longed to be her teacher and through her to transmit his intellectual legacy to posterity. However, she refused his proposal of marriage, just as she had already refused a proposal from Rée.

The chapel on the summit of the Sacro Monte at Orta, which Nietzsche and Lou von Salomé climbed in May 1882.

Trying to ignore their emotional tensions, the three formed an intellectual group. Over the summer of 1882 they moved from Rome to the Italian lakes and thence to Lucerne. At Orta, near Stresa on Lake Maggiore, Lou and Nietzsche climbed a hill called Sacro Monte, the Sacred Mountain. Whatever happened (or didn't happen) there, it was for Nietzsche a very special moment. When they descended, he said quietly to Lou: 'I thank you for the most exquisite dream of my life.'[3] Rée, however, became suspicious and jealous. At Lucerne, Nietzsche insisted that they should visit a photographer's studio and have themselves photographed. The famous photograph shows Nietzsche and Rée drawing a cart on which Lou is crouching with a whip in her hand. Rée had a morbid dislike of having his picture taken, and his reluctance is unmistakable.

Tensions mounted when the three went to Bayreuth and met the Wagners and Elisabeth Nietzsche. Lou naively felt that Elisabeth

1882.

Photograph of Lou von Salomé in a cart drawn by Nietzsche and Paul Rée, taken in a studio in Lucerne, summer 1882.

was practically her own sister, but Elisabeth, feeling possessive towards her beloved brother and unable to share his and Lou's intellectual interests, considered Lou a dangerous rival and also an immoral and irresponsible flirt. Nietzsche, Elisabeth and Lou spent most of August in the village of Tautenburg outside Jena. Elisabeth quarrelled with Lou, and Nietzsche wrote that every five days he and Lou had 'a little tragic scene' (to Köselitz, 20 August 1882). In October, Nietzsche, Lou and Rée were together in Leipzig. Although the trinity felt increasingly fragile, they still made vague plans to reassemble in Paris, and Nietzsche wrote to a friend in Paris to arrange accommodation. On 5 November, however, Rée and Lou left Leipzig together, and soon Nietzsche realized that the trinity was dissolved for good. He never saw either Rée or Lou again.

The disappointment Nietzsche had suffered – all the more bitter because he had so much idealized Lou – was the kind of experience one recovers from only slowly, if at all. To make matters worse, his solitary lifestyle left him free to brood about it obsessively. He came to realize that Elisabeth had manipulated him into disliking Lou; he felt that Rée had alienated him from Lou by slandering him; and Lou herself seemed not the radiant free spirit he had imagined, but, as he wrote in a terrible letter to Rée's brother, 'a dried-up dirty evil-smelling she-ape with her false breasts' (to Georg Rée, mid-July 1883). For a time he was estranged from his mother and sister. 'I think I have endured more, five times more, than would suffice to drive a normal person to suicide; and it is not yet over,' he wrote to the sympathetic Ida Overbeck (mid-July 1883).

A letter to his sister of 29 August 1883 suggests, however, that after many epistolary outbursts over the preceding months, he has now constructed a narrative that makes acceptable sense of the Lou–Rée episode. Lou and Rée were wholly different from him, but they were at least 'original people, not copies; that is why I put up with them, however much they offended my taste'. However, they diverted him from his true path, to which illness

Nietzsche, September 1882, photograph by Gustav Schulze, Naumburg.

has now brought him back: 'the entire meaning of the physical pains to which I was exposed is that they alone pulled me out of a conception of my life's work that was wrong, that is, a hundred times too *low*.' The teachers of his youth, Schopenhauer and Wagner, were likewise of merely transient significance, enabling him to perceive an ideal that now renders them superfluous. This process of overcoming past influences is recorded, he continues, in his new book, *Thus Spoke Zarathustra*: 'Every word of my Zarathustra is victorious mockery and more than mockery directed against the ideals of that time; and behind almost every word stands a personal experience, a self-overcoming of the first rank' (29 August 1883). In the light of this letter, we might want to read *Zarathustra* as a disguised personal confession. No doubt it is in part, but it must be understood first and foremost as a work of lyrical and dramatic philosophy which communicates with the reader independently of its author's biography.

Thus Spoke Zarathustra

After the catastrophic break-up of his relations with Lou and Rée, in November 1882 Nietzsche went to Rapallo, and on 1 February 1883 he told Köselitz that he had written a small book, with cathartic effect: 'I have rolled away a heavy stone from my soul.' This was Part One of *Zarathustra*; Nietzsche claims to have written it in only ten days, and later in *Ecce Homo* he asserts that Parts Two and Three were also written in ten days each. They were published separately between August 1883 and April 1884. In the winter of 1884–5 he wrote Part Four, of which he had only forty copies printed; he gave nine of these to friends.

The prophet Zarathustra is named after Zoroaster, the founder of the ancient Iranian religion. He feels a special affinity with the sun, which the Zoroastrians worshipped (z Prologue 1). He also has traits of the Buddha, and the language of his speeches is heavily indebted to Luther's translation of the Bible, with which Nietzsche, the son of a Lutheran clergyman, was deeply familiar.

The action of the book is slight. At the age of thirty, Zarathustra leaves his home town and retires to a cave in the mountains, where he spends ten years in the company only of an eagle and a serpent. Then he descends to the town called 'The Motley Cow' (a translation of Kalmasadalmya, the name of a town which the Buddha is said to have visited).[4] However, nobody listens to his message, so he returns to his cave for some years before re-emerging and sailing to the Fortunate Isles, where his friends and disciples live.[5] After preaching there, he resolves to return to his cave, so he sails home and travels by an indirect route to The Motley Cow and thence to his cave, where he falls ill and is tended by his animals. More time passes; Zarathustra's hair grows white; then in Part Four he is visited by a number of strange characters, including two kings, the last pope and 'the ugliest man', collectively called 'the highest men'. Even they do not seem ready for Zarathustra's revelation, for they regress to religion and fall to worshipping a donkey. All flee on the appearance of a lion, whom Zarathustra greets as a sign that he can resume his mission with better prospects. There the narrative ends; Nietzsche never carried out his plan to write a fifth and sixth part.

The real action is internal, consisting in Zarathustra's repeated struggle to overcome disappointment and despair. His preaching on the Fortunate Isles is interrupted by three lyrical sections. In 'The Night-Song' he laments that his intense love of humanity means that he always gives and never receives. In 'The Dance-Song', when he and his disciples find some girls dancing in a glade, he sings to them an apostrophe to the feminine figures of Life and Wisdom, but afterwards he is still sad. Pursuing this emotion, he sails to the Isle of the Graves, where he reflects on his many disappointments and the frustration imposed on him by his enemies. However, he still has his indomitable will, and he concludes: 'hail to thee, my will! And only where there are graves are there resurrections.' After this successful confrontation with despair, the next section is appropriately 'On Self-Overcoming': Life confides to Zarathustra, 'Behold, I am *that which must always overcome itself*.'

Zarathustra must go through further trials. At the end of Book Two his self-knowledge tells him that he is not yet mature enough for his own ideals ('The Stillest Hour'). Weeping bitterly, he leaves his disciples and returns home. Soon after arriving, he is overcome by an 'abyss-deep thought' (III 13): he faints, lies for some time as though dead, and then remains helpless for seven days. When he recovers, his attendant animals tell him that he is destined to be 'the teacher of the Eternal Recurrence'; this – as we shall see, extremely problematic – doctrine is presumably the 'abyss-deep thought' that prostrated him.[6]

Zarathustra's Teaching

Many of Zarathustra's doctrines are recognizable from Nietzsche's more conventional books. What his disciples make of them, we cannot tell, because the disciples never appear as individuals. Zarathustra only rarely interacts with other people. Most of the book consists of his prophetic monologues. His values, as one would expect, are the antithesis of Christian values. Where Christianity blames evil on man's desire to eat of the tree of knowledge, Zarathustra commends knowledge; that is one reason why his faithful companions include 'the serpent of knowledge' (I 22/1). Zarathustra is filled with love for humanity – 'My impatient love overflows in torrents, downward, towards rising and setting' (II 1) – but it is not Christian love: its object is not present-day humans, but what humanity may become. His 'bestowing virtue' is challenging, demanding and dangerous (I 22). Where Christianity inculcates love of one's neighbour (*Nächstenliebe*), Zarathustra advocates 'love of the farthest' (*Fernsten-Liebe*, I 16): he wants people to look beyond the present and imagine the future of humanity. Similarly, they are to get beyond short-sighted patriotic love of the fatherland and love the future *'children's land'* (II 14). Christianity advocates forgiving one's enemies, but in doing so one makes one's enemies feel ashamed; instead, one should show them that they have inadvertently conferred a benefit on one (I 19).[7] Christianity denounces *'sensuality, the lust to rule, selfishness'*, but Zarathustra reclaims them ('On the Three Evils', III 10). Only the dirty-minded disapprove of sensuality, which is a source of happiness. The lust to rule is necessary for rulers who aim to improve the human race. And Zarathustra's 'bestowing virtue' is compatible with 'the wholesome, healthy selfishness that wells up from a powerful soul'. All these qualities will be properly acknowledged when Zarathustra's teaching is generally accepted: here and elsewhere Zarathustra prophesies *'the Great Midday'*, the noontide when all shadows are dispelled by what Nietzsche earlier called 'the sunshine of knowledge' (*ws* preface).

Along with Christian values, Zarathustra denounces many tendencies which Nietzsche disliked in the nineteenth century. The state is condemned as the 'new idol' that has displaced peoples and nations and exists merely to satisfy the ambitions of 'superfluous creatures' (I 11). The state encourages the 'preachers of death' who are later compared to tarantulas, poisonous spiders, because they preach equality but are really motivated by envy and vindictiveness ('On the Tarantulas').[8] The cultural and educational ideal (*Bildung*) of the nineteenth century, which thanks to historical learning is able to draw eclectically on all past cultures, is derided as a motley display without substance, like the rags of a scarecrow: 'If one could remove your veils and wraps and colours and gestures, there would be just enough left over to frighten away the birds' ('On the Land of Culture').

Zarathustra on Women

Zarathustra has strong views about women, and since they are consistent with the disapproval Nietzsche expresses elsewhere for female emancipation, the question of Nietzsche and feminism may best be considered here. One of the few dialogues in *Zarathustra* is with a little old woman, who ends by telling Zarathustra 'a little truth', namely the notorious injunction: 'You are going to women? Then don't forget the whip!' ('On Old and Young Little Women' I 18). Some readers, regarding Nietzsche as an emancipatory writer, have tried hard to read him against the grain and find a pro-feminist message concealed in his writings.[9] His explicit and unmistakable message, however, is that women are naturally subordinate to men and should be kept in subjection. A 'wise man' says: 'Man's nature is will, woman's nature is willingness – that is the law of the sexes, truly! A hard law for woman!' (*GS* 68). From the early 1880s onwards, the hint of sympathy here vanishes and Nietzsche's misogyny hardens. Zarathustra tells the old woman (who agrees): 'the happiness of a man is: I will. The happiness of a woman is: he wills.' Women are an enigma, but all their problems can be solved by pregnancy. They regard men only as an instrument to help produce a child. To men, women are dangerous playthings. Men's emotions are deep, women's are shallow (see *GS* 60–72).

Elsewhere Nietzsche applies this outlook to nineteenth-century society. The emancipation of women merely unfits them for their proper business, which is to make men's lives easier. They need to be kept down by fear of men (*BGE* 232). Greeks and orientals had the right idea when they treated women as their property and locked them away (*BGE* 238). Nowadays, when women have access to education, and even read newspapers and talk politics, they are losing their femininity (*BGE* 239). A women who seeks learning generally has something wrong with her sexuality (*BGE* 144). George Eliot (whose work Nietzsche did not know at first hand) is a 'little moral female' who has failed to shake off Christian morality (*TI* 'Expeditions' 5). George Sand is an insufferable, pretentious, self-satisfied 'writing cow' (*Schreibe-Kuh*, *TI* 'Expeditions' 6) under the bad influence of Rousseau.

The extreme misogyny of Nietzsche's writings is the more surprising since he had several close friendships with intellectual women. As we have seen, he had a warm and affectionate relationship with the feminist Malwida von Meysenbug. Several of Nietzsche's female friends, including Lou von Salomé, had studied at Zurich when German universities were still closed to women. Nietzsche even voted in 1875 to admit women to the conservative University of Basel, although the proposal was defeated by six votes to four. Among his friends, Resa von Schirnhofer (1855–1948) and Meta von Salis (1855–1929) had gained doctorates in philosophy; Helene von Druskowitz (1856–1918) had written a doctoral thesis on Byron.[10] The forthright Druskowitz was the only one who challenged Nietzsche's ideas in print; he was not pleased, and referred to her as a 'little literature-goose' (to Carl Spitteler, 17 September 1887). In 1885 Nietzsche reports to his sister that the female students in Zurich have gradually discovered that he is against women's emancipation, and are furious with him (7 May 1885). Yet Meta von Salis reports that he often talked about women who had distinguished themselves, and in his last (sane) letter to her he informs her that the Russian mathematician Sofya Kovalevskaya (1850–1891) has received the Paris Academy's highest award for mathematics (29 December 1888). All witnesses agree that in person Nietzsche treated women with unfailing courtesy and consideration.

The discrepancy between Nietzsche's personal behaviour and his misogyny in print is puzzling. His rejection by Lou von Salomé does not completely account for it. The sentence about the whip is difficult to explain away. It must be associated somehow with the photograph which shows Nietzsche and Rée pulling a cart on which Salomé is standing and waving a whip. Attempts have been made to soften the notorious sentence: Nietzsche's sister claimed that it went back to a private joke suggested by an incident in Turgenev's story *First Love*, which she read aloud to him in 1882; others have maintained that the whole passage is a self-caricature, or that the whip might be the woman's, as in the photograph.[11] It seems that despite his female friends, Nietzsche at his desk regarded the growing women's movement as yet another of the nineteenth-century tendencies that he deplored as signs of degeneration.[12]

After the Death of God

Equality, feminism, socialism, democracy, subjection to the state: if these tendencies continue, Zarathustra foresees humanity declining into 'the last humans' – people with no ideals beyond comfort and the avoidance of pain, who think that they have invented happiness (Prologue 5). The 'last humans' will inhabit a post-Christian universe, as Zarathustra does. They live after the death of God. The only person who has not yet heard the news of God's death is a pious old hermit whom Zarathustra meets in the depths of the forest (Prologue 2). But the 'last humans' have discarded Christian ideals without finding any other ideals. They represent nineteenth-century conceptions of political equality and material welfare taken to the extreme. 'Everyone wants the same thing, everyone is the same: whoever feels differently goes voluntarily to the madhouse' (Prologue 5).

Zarathustra draws different conclusions from the death of God. Not only is there no God, there is no 'other world', no transcendent world somehow lurking behind this one. Zarathustra calls such a notion 'a world behind' (*Hinterwelt*), and its devotees are *Hinterweltler* (1 3: a pun on *Hinterwäldler*, 'backwoodsmen'). They despise this world and the body, pretending that suffering here will lead to happiness beyond, but they are 'poisoners' and 'despisers of life'. Zarathustra repeatedly and fervently enjoins his followers: *stay true to the earth* and do not believe those who talk of over-earthly hopes!' (Prologue 3; cf. 1 22).

Just as he rejects Christianity's claim that there is a next world superior to this one, Zarathustra denies that we have a soul which is superior to the body. To say that one is divided into soul and body is childish: 'the awakened one, the one who knows, says: Body am I through and through, and nothing besides; and soul is merely a word for something about the body' (1 4). Moreover, Zarathustra continues, it is wrong to imagine 'reason' (*Vernunft*) as a distinct faculty located in the mind and directing the mindless body:

> The body is a great reason, a manifold with one sense,
> a war and a peace, a herd and a herdsman.
> A tool of the body is your small reason, too, my brother, which
> you call 'spirit', a small tool and toy of your great reason. (1 4)

The body knows better than the spirit or mind what is good for one. By obeying the commands of the body, one can ensure one's physical well-being, which is the basis of all other well-being. This emphasis on the body reminds us that *Zarathustra* is the work of a chronically sick man who had carefully to monitor his own diet and whose travels around Europe were dictated by his extreme sensitivity to climate. It prepares us for the immense, almost obsessive importance that Nietzsche's subsequent publications attach to physiology. Thus he affirms in *Twilight of the Idols* that culture requires above all the cultivation of the body:

> It is decisive for the fortunes of nations and of mankind that one should inaugurate culture in the *right place* – *not* in the 'soul' (as has been the fateful superstition of priests and quasi-priests): the right place is the body, demeanour, diet, physiology: the *rest* follows . . . This is why the Greeks remain the *supreme cultural event* of history – they knew, they *did* what needed to

be done; Christianity, which despised the body, has up till now been mankind's greatest misfortune. (*TI* 'Expeditions' 47)

Zarathustra urges us to shake off the otherworldly fantasies and the ascetic self-mortification that Christianity has imposed. We should appreciate the actual world in which we live with our bodies. In place of religious gloom, Zarathustra advocates laughter and dancing. His version of the Devil is the 'Spirit of Heaviness' who forbids people to love themselves and persuades them that life is a burden (III 11). Zarathustra responds by praising physical activity in which the body becomes light and which should ideally culminate in flying: 'this is my teaching: whoever wants to learn to fly must first learn to stand and walk and run and climb and dance – one cannot fly into flying!' (III 11).

The ideal that Zarathustra preaches most enthusiastically is the affirmation of life. He associates it with the sun and the sky, which he apostrophizes as 'O Heaven above me, so pure! so deep! You light-abyss!' (III 4). This affirmation is not facile, but has cost him much pain: 'A blesser I have become and a Yea-sayer: and for that I struggled long and was a wrestler, that I might one day wrest my hands free for blessing' (III 4). Having learned to bless, he has learned that the supreme activity is creation. The creator is 'the one who creates humanity's goal and gives the earth its sense and its future: he alone *makes it that* anything is good or evil' (III 12/2).

It seems a pity to translate Zarathustra's exalted poetic prose into the inevitably flat language of philosophical exposition. Nevertheless, the attempt must be made, for in *Zarathustra* Nietzsche broaches three concepts that have generally been thought central to his later philosophy: the Overhuman (Übermensch), the eternal recurrence and the will to power.

The Overhuman

No transcendence is needed to give earthly life a meaning and purpose. The meaning and purpose of life, Zarathustra proclaims, are centred on the Übermensch.[13]

> *I teach to you the Overhuman.* The human is something that shall be overcome. What have you done to overcome it? [. . .] What is the ape for the human being? A laughing-stock or a painful cause for shame. And the human shall be just that for the Overhuman: a laughing-stock or a painful cause for shame. (Prologue 3)

Present-day humanity represents a transition from the animal to the Overhuman, 'a rope, fastened between beast and Overhuman' (Prologue 4). Humans have developed from worms and from apes, and much in us still embarrassingly recalls the ape.

These passages may seem to imply that the Overhuman represents a future stage in evolution. As we saw in the last chapter, Nietzsche broadly accepted evolutionary theory, although he had many reservations about the Darwinian version. Are we to think that Zarathustra is prophesying a future super-race? Later, in *Ecce Homo*, Nietzsche will indignantly disclaim the suggestion that the Overhuman has anything to do with Darwinism (*EH* 'Books' 1). There he explains that the Overhuman is a supremely healthy human type ('Typus höchster Wohlgeratenheit', ibid.).

Given the importance Nietzsche attaches to the individual, it is unlikely that he envisaged humanity as a whole evolving into a superior race. His Overhuman is much more likely to be a member of an elite, composed of highly developed individuals.[14] He offers us two accounts of the Overhuman, which are not necessarily incompatible; they may be different aspects of the same being. The Overhuman will be the antithesis of degenerate nineteenth-century humanity. In contrast to democratic herd animals, he will be an individual. He will be healthy, completely free from the sickness implanted by Christianity. He will be noble and generous. He may pass through 'the three transformations of the spirit' memorably evoked early in *Zarathustra*. The strong spirit is at first a camel, eagerly bearing burdens. Then the spirit is transformed into a lion; the lion, like the camel, inhabits the desert, but his aggressive nature enables him to confront the great dragon 'Thou shalt', the embodiment of moral coercion. The lion's motto is 'I will'; he does not obey external laws or commands, but uses his freedom to create his own values. Having defeated the dragon, the lion becomes a child – a being who is innocent, beyond good and evil, who plays creatively, participating in what Nietzsche later calls 'the innocence of becoming' (*TI* 'Errors' 8), and who affirms life: 'Yes, for the play of creating, my brothers, a sacred Yea-saying is needed: the spirit now wills *its own* will, the one who had lost the world attains *its own* world' (*Z* 1 1). This would justify the appealing interpretation of the Overhuman as one who 'has overcome his animal nature, organized the chaos of his passions, sublimated his impulses'.[15] To that extent the Overhuman has a partial precursor in one of Nietzsche's heroes, Goethe, 'a spirit who *became* free' (*TI* 'Expeditions' 49).

Other attributes of the Overhuman, however, make the above description of him seem sanitized. The Overhuman will be masculine and enjoy warfare (*GS* 362). He has precursors in the tyrants who emerged in the ancient world and who were the first individuals (*GS* 23), such as Alexander, Alcibiades and Julius Caesar. In Burckhardt's *Civilization of the Renaissance in Italy*, Nietzsche found further models. Burckhardt's Renaissance is typified by tyrants who seized power and who, lacking traditional legitimacy, had to develop a calculating, objective and amoral outlook in order to survive. They too were individuals, as were their associates. They had a precursor in the Hohenstaufen emperor Frederick II (1194–1250), whom Burckhardt calls 'the first ruler of the modern type',[16] and Nietzsche 'an atheist and enemy of the Church *comme il faut*' (*EH* 'z' 4). Their supreme example was Cesare Borgia, whom Machiavelli praised in *The Prince*; Burckhardt finds Cesare remarkable for 'the very excess of his wickedness',[17] but Nietzsche praises him unreservedly (to Meysenbug, 20 October 1888). These people embody happiness, understood as follows:

> What is happiness? – The feeling that power
> *grows*, that a resistance is overcome.
> *Not* contentment, but more power; *not* peace at all, but
> war; *not* virtue, but competence (virtue in Renaissance
> style, virtù, without an injection of moralism.) (*A* 2)

The Renaissance found an heir in Napoleon (*GS* 362), who was a synthesis of '*Unmensch* [monster] and Overhuman' (*GM* I 16). Such people know how to command. In future they may form a hereditary aristocracy whose authority will be accepted unquestioningly by their subjects (*GS* 40). To develop Nietzsche's imagery, nineteenth-century Europe is ruled by sheep, who have put lions in cages where they waste away; but in future the lions, the natural aristocrats among animals, will break free, regain their strength and beauty, and have no compassion for the sheep.

The meaning and purpose of life are not to be found in any external authority; they are immanent in life itself. They consist in the development of the full potential of humanity – that is, of the select minority of humans who are capable of becoming Overhumans. Nobody else matters. This is the centre of Zarathustra's teaching, associated with the image of noonday when the sun shines straight down on the redeemed earth: '"*Dead are all Gods*: now we want the Overhuman to live" – may this be at the Great Midday our ultimate will!' (I 22).

The Eternal Recurrence

One of the most famous but most obscure doctrines formulated in *Zarathustra* is the eternal recurrence. Nietzsche tells us that the idea suddenly occurred to him one day in August 1881 when he was walking beside Lake Silvaplana, near Sils Maria, and stopped under a certain pyramid-shaped rock (*EH* 'z' 1). Curiously, however, this idea, which Nietzsche in 1888 describes as the 'basic conception' of *Zarathustra* (ibid.), does not appear until more than halfway through the text. Zarathustra expresses it as part of a vision, which he recounts to sailors during his voyage from the Fortunate Isles. Later the doctrine is formulated for him by his animals, who tell Zarathustra that he is destined to be 'the teacher of the Eternal Recurrence' (III 13/2).

In Zarathustra's vision, he arrives, in the company of a cynical dwarf, at a gateway where two roads meet. Each road, the one behind and the one in front, stretches for an eternity. The gateway where they meet is the moment. All things must already have gone along the road behind Zarathustra, and must in future pass along the road in front of him.

> For whatever among all things *can* walk: in this
> long lane *out*, too – it *must* walk once more!
> And this slow-moving spider, crawling in the
> moonlight, and the moonlight itself, and I and you in
> the gateway, whispering together, whispering of eternal
> things – must we not all have been here before?
> and must come again and walk in that other lane, out
> there, before us, in this long and dreadful lane – must
> we not eternally come back again? (*Z* III 2)

This haunting passage gains its force from the mysterious setting; from the sharply focused detail of the spider crawling

The rock beside Lake Silvaplana, where Nietzsche conceived the idea of the Eternal Recurrence in August 1881.

in the moonlight; and from being a dialogue, whereas most of Zarathustra's speeches are monologues. Initially, the prospect of all things happening again and again forever seems horrific. It is alleviated by the next part of Zarathustra's vision, in which a snake crawls down a young man's throat while he is sleeping, but he wakes, bites its head off, and is reinvigorated and laughs. His laughter tells Zarathustra that it is possible to absorb the hardest doctrine – even that of the eternal recurrence – and feel a new kind of joy.

Zarathustra's animals present the doctrine more positively. They assert that there is a 'Great Year' which comes to its end and starts again, like an hourglass being reversed. Zarathustra should therefore say:

I come again, with this sun, with this earth, with this eagle, with
this serpent – *not* to a new life or a better life or a similar life;
I come eternally again to this self-same life, in the
greatest and smallest respects, so that again I teach
the eternal recurrence of all things. (*z* III 13)

Is this doctrine a theory about the nature of the cosmos? Or is
it a moral test to see whether one can endure an overwhelming
possibility? The most important expression of the idea elsewhere
in Nietzsche's published works occurs late in Book IV of *The
Gay Science*, which was published in August 1882, and so was
presumably written not very long after the moment of revelation at
Lake Silvaplana. It is headed 'The Heaviest Weight' and imagines
that in one's utmost solitude one might be informed by a demon
that one would have to live one's life again, experiencing all
pleasures and pains and everything down to the smallest detail,
not just once more but innumerable times. The images of the spider
in the moonlight and the 'eternal hour-glass of existence' reappear
here. One might react with horror, cursing the demon; or, in a
supreme moment, one might be able to reply to the demon: 'You are
a god and I have never heard anything more divine!' (*GS* 341)

Here the eternal recurrence appears primarily as a moral
test. If one can accept with joy the prospect of reliving one's life
repeatedly, one has shown one's ability to affirm life. But the
test would lack any force if it were based on a mere fancy, and if
the eternal recurrence were a mere thought-experiment which
committed one to nothing. The demon presents his suggestion
vividly and powerfully, and the possibility of the eternal recurrence
is portrayed as an extreme challenge.

Some commentators think that Nietzsche is restating the theory
found among Greek philosophers that the world is repeatedly
destroyed and renewed.[18] Thus the pre-Socratic thinkers
Anaximander and Heraclitus both thought that the world is

periodically destroyed in fire and and then reborn; the Platonic tradition imagined that after a Great Year, lasting some 36,000 ordinary years, the heavenly bodies would return to their present alignments and history would repeat itself.[19] Zarathustra's animals speak of 'a Great Year of Becoming, a monster of a Great Year' (III 13/2). But this recalls the Platonic year only as a small-scale analogy to something greater. Besides, as Nietzsche was already familiar with these ideas, they would not have struck him with the force of a revelation. When he talked about the eternal recurrence to Lou von Salomé in 1882, he spoke of it 'only in a low voice and with every sign of the deepest horror'.[20]

There is ample evidence that Nietzsche took the eternal recurrence seriously as a cosmological theory, placed on a new foundation by modern physics. His notebooks for 1881 contain notes on thermodynamics, which he learned about especially from Lange's *History of Materialism*. He formulates the law of the conservation of energy: 'The world of forces suffers no diminution' (*KSA* IX 498). If energy is constant, and if, as Nietzsche took for granted, the universe is infinite in duration, it follows that during infinite time the components of the universe must undergo all possible changes and return to their original pattern – only then to undergo all possible changes once more, and so on *ad infinitum*. Nietzsche also read in Lange about the second law of thermodynamics, which says that energy achieves a state of equilibrium inside a closed system, therefore heat will reach an equilibrium and the universe will perish in heat-death; but he argues in his notebooks that, given that time is infinite, a state of equilibrium would have been reached long before now, so the second law must be mistaken. Nietzsche's cosmology was based on assumptions that are now outdated. Not only has the second law of thermodynamics been upheld by modern physics, but it is now agreed that the universe, far from being infinite in duration, originated from the Big Bang, some 15 billion years ago; cosmologists differ as to whether the universe will continue expanding indefinitely, or whether it will ultimately collapse back on itself and come to an end in some unimaginably distant future.[21]

However, Nietzsche does not seem concerned with cosmology for its own sake. In his published writings, he concentrates on the moral consequences of the eternal recurrence for the individual. He ignores the implication that all history's wars, massacres, plagues and natural disasters will keep recurring forever. Nor does he explore its dizzying further implications.[22] Although he is fascinated by the theory, he does not seem very interested in it.

As Nietzsche presents it, the eternal recurrence challenges the individual to say in effect, 'Yes, despite everything, life is worth living, and I would willingly go through it all again.' It recalls the concept of *amor fati* (love of fate) with which Nietzsche formulates his New Year's resolution for 1882:

> Amor fati: henceforth let that be my love! I do not wish
> to wage war against what is ugly. I do not wish to accuse,
> I do not wish even to accuse the accusers. Let *looking
> away* be my only negation! And, all things considered on
> a large scale: I wish only to be a Yea-sayer! (*GS* 276)

Yet *amor fati*, like Nietzsche's earlier rejoinder to 'Turkish fatalism' (*WS* 61), seems to be a passive acceptance of necessity, whereas the eternal recurrence demands an energetic affirmation. And here it presents moral as well as cosmological problems. It has been understood as an injunction to act in such a way that I could wish my act to be repeated eternally.[23] But it carries the discouraging implication that whatever I choose to do, I have already done it in all my previous lives: so is my choice real? Or it may be read as affirming the infinite value of the moment, as in Zarathustra's 'Other Dance-Song': 'For all joy wants – eternity!' (*Z* III 15/3).[24] Yet if the doctrine is true, then the moment is not unique, but will be repeated innumerable times; and it is not only joy that is eternal, but pain, boredom, depression. One might also object that my previous and future lives, if they exist, are so remote that they cannot possibly matter to me; or that the 'me' of past and future lives is not actually me, but a double, whom I need not care about.[25]

The idea of the eternal recurrence was very important to Nietzsche, judging from the many references to it in his notebooks; he used to confide it to acquaintances as a solemn secret.[26] Yet it makes remarkably few appearances in his published writings: once in *The Gay Science*, twice in *Zarathustra*, plus a brief mention in *Twilight of the Idols*. Zarathustra may be destined to teach the eternal recurrence, but he never gets round to doing so. Neither does Nietzsche, although he calls himself 'the teacher of the Eternal Recurrence' (*TI* 'Ancients' 5). So it is strange for Nietzsche to claim that it formed the 'basic conception' of *Zarathustra*, and for Andreas-Salomé (the name she used after her marriage in 1887) to maintain that it is the 'foundation and crown of his intellectual edifice'.[27] These assertions have often been accepted unquestioningly, but we know that authors who give retrospective interpretations of their own works are not always reliable. It is possible that Nietzsche thought of including the eternal recurrence in *Zarathustra* only when halfway through writing the book. Alternatively, it may be that Zarathustra's teachings in Books One and Two are to be understood only as a prelude to his most challenging message, that of the eternal recurrence, and that at the end of Book Four the reinvigorated Zarathustra is setting out to teach it, and would have done so if Nietzsche had written Books Five and Six.[28] If so, however, it is curious that in 1884, having completed Book Three, he announces that *Zarathustra* is now 'complete in its three Acts' (to Rohde, 22 February 1884); and that in the section of *Ecce Homo* dealing with *Zarathustra* Nietzsche says nothing about any plan for continuing it, and does not even mention that the book is incomplete.

Zarathustra is presented as the supreme exponent of affirming life, saying 'yes' to life. Thanks in part to Nietzsche's influence, 'life-affirming' is now a term of praise. But what does it mean to affirm or even accept life? To affirm life must mean saying that life is good. But Nietzsche has already told us that life is neither good nor the reverse: it is beyond good and evil. The affirmation of life therefore cannot be a response to the nature of life, but is an exercise of the philosopher's will. Anyway, if I accept life or the universe, that makes no difference to the universe. William James tells a relevant anecdote:

> 'I accept the universe' is reported to have been a favorite utterance of our New England transcendentalist, Margaret Fuller; and when some one repeated this phrase to Thomas Carlyle, his sardonic comment is said to have been 'Gad! she'd better!'[29]

Accepting or affirming life, however, may matter a great deal, not to the universe, but to me. Hence Nietzsche's call for affirmation has been interpreted as an injunction to affirm *oneself*. I should be able to affirm all of my experiences, even my sufferings, disappointments and pains, because they have helped to make me who I am.[30]

However, Nietzsche seems to mean more than that, if we look at his last published reference to the eternal recurrence in the closing section of *Twilight of the Idols*. Here Nietzsche, describing himself as 'the teacher of the Eternal Recurrence', advocates the 'affirmation of life even in its strangest and sternest problems' (*TI* 'Ancients' 5), but explains that such affirmation is tragic. The will to life rejoices when its highest products (its noblest people) are sacrificed, like the heroes in tragedy, and it does so because life has such inexhaustible fullness that it can afford the loss and also takes pleasure in destruction as well as in creation. Tragic affirmation wishes '*to be oneself* the eternal joy of becoming': to identify with the eternal flux of things. One not only says yes to life, but feels oneself to be part of the cosmic process, a play of energy that is profoundly satisfying in itself with no need for any ultimate purpose.

Yet is such affirmation anything more than an affirmative *feeling*? In a particularly buoyant mood, one may feel that 'yes, life is good, despite everything,' and may project that feeling as a conception of the cosmos. But a feeling is not a doctrine. One cannot teach a feeling or persuade people to have it. Considered as a proposition, the claim that life should be affirmed runs up against the fact, which we have seen stressed by Schopenhauer, that the suffering in life far outweighs the pleasure. That includes not only human suffering, but the suffering of animals in a world where one species lives by devouring another. I may affirm my own suffering, but what right have I to affirm the suffering of innumerable other sentient beings? Yet that is what 'saying yes to life' entails. Given the predominance of pain, the 'anti-natalist' philosopher David Benatar has argued, cogently, that existence is an evil and that it would be better never to have been born – the wisdom of Silenus, now placed on a logical foundation.[31]

If one still wishes to affirm life, one does not need the hypothesis of the eternal recurrence. It may take just as much resolution to affirm life even though every moment is unique, transitory and unrepeatable. At all events, the eternal recurrence, far from being central to Nietzsche's philosophy, seems, on examination, to be inessential and even marginal to it. Nothing else in Nietzsche's thought *depends* on the eternal recurrence. Nevertheless, Nietzsche continued to attach great importance to the idea; most of his plans for a magnum opus envisage a final and culminating section dealing with the eternal recurrence.

The Will to Power

The concept of the will to power, introduced in *Zarathustra*, recurs throughout Nietzsche's subsequent writings. A discussion of it here will form a bridge to the later texts and illuminate the problems with it, while the next chapter will look at the uses Nietzsche makes of it in explaining human psychology and history in concrete instances.

Zarathustra gives an address to philosophers who profess to be motivated by the will to truth. What they really want, he says, is to make the world thinkable – that is, to reduce it to fit their impoverished conception of truth. This endeavour is egoistic: they want the world to reflect themselves. Hence it is not driven by any impersonal will to truth, but by a self-centred will to power. However, it is bound to fail. For as their little boat sails along the river of life (the eternal flux that is reality), they are at the mercy of life itself, which is equivalent to will to power. Zarathustra adjures them:

> Now hear my word, you who are wisest! Test in
> earnest whether I have crept into the very heart
> of Life, and into the very roots of her heart!
> Where I found the living, there I found will to power; and even
> in the will of one who serves I found a will to be master.
> That the weaker should serve the stronger, of this it is
> persuaded by its will, which would be master over what is
> weaker still: this pleasure alone it does not gladly forgo. (II 12)

Yet the will to power is not only directed against other people, but, primarily, against oneself. One has to overcome one's present self for the sake of one's future self. Life, as we have seen, consists in self-overcoming. This concept is illustrated elsewhere in *Zarathustra* by the protagonist's acceptance of the initially repellent eternal recurrence, figured in the young shepherd's biting off the head of the snake. In *Beyond Good and Evil* Nietzsche declares roundly 'life as such is will to power' (*BGE* 13), and offers this as a possible comprehensive explanation of all action:

> Granted finally that one succeeded in explaining our entire instinctual life as the development and ramification of *one* basic form of will – as will to power, as in *my* theory –; granted that one could trace all organic functions back to this will to power and could also find in it the solution to the problem of procreation and nourishment – they are *one* problem – one would have acquired the right to define *all* efficient force unequivocally as: *will to power*. (*BGE* 36)

Applied to human existence, this has drastic consequences: 'life itself is *essentially* appropriation, injury, overpowering of the strange and weaker, suppression, severity, imposition of one's own forms, incorporation and, at the least and mildest, exploitation' (*BGE* 259). A healthy aristocracy will behave in such ways to its inferiors:

> [it] must, if it is a living and not a decaying body, itself do all that to other bodies which the individuals within it refrain from doing to each other: it will have to be the will to power incarnate, it will want to grow, expand, draw to itself, gain ascendancy – not out of any morality or immorality, but because it *lives*, and because life *is* will to power. (Ibid.)

This theory of the will to power is not easy to reconcile with the determinism that Nietzsche emphatically maintained in *Human, All-Too-Human*. For if my actions are determined, I can hardly be said to be exercising my will. At most I can have a *feeling* of power, which Nietzsche thinks is the greatest source of happiness (*D* 356, *GM* III 7). But Nietzsche wants to go further and maintain that the will to power motivates *actions*: it is the 'path to power, to action, to the most powerful action' (*GM* III 7). He seems to have softened his determinism into the much less controversial contention that people act in accordance with their characters. There is no point in telling a strong creature, like an eagle or a Renaissance tyrant, not to prey on weak ones, because there is no neutral inner self which could *choose* to be either strong or weak, and therefore it is impossible to choose between one form of behaviour and another (*GM* I 13).

Nietzsche was encouraged to use the concept of 'will to power' by his reading in natural science. Reading the argument by the physicist Maximilian Drossbach that force is really 'the striving for expansion', Nietzsche wrote in the margin: 'I say will to power.'[32] Biology provided further support: Nietzsche was particularly taken by the claims made by Wilhelm Roux that organs, cells and even molecules within an organism were in constant competition, in which the stronger gained command over the weaker.[33] However, Nietzsche applied the concept to human motivation and activity, and indeed increasingly employed it as 'the single explanation for all occurrences in the organic and inorganic realms'.[34]

The all-embracing theory of the will to power enabled Nietzsche to envisage the universe as constantly active. It thus supported his opposition to materialism and mechanism. We have already seen that he rejected classical atomism, according to which the world was composed of material particles that randomly coalesced to form larger entities; he preferred Boscovich's theory that the components of reality were not substances but forces (*BGE* 12). He also rejected the scientific materialism that enjoyed high prestige in the later nineteenth century: it was reductive, and could at most describe natural processes, not explain them.

It remains unclear what kind of theory Nietzsche is offering instead. Are we to understand the will to power as an empirical concept or as a metaphysical one? Applied to human life, it may be seen as a powerful tool with which Nietzsche continues the psychological analyses begun in *Human, All-Too-Human*, and I will argue in the next chapter that he uses it in this way in *The Genealogy of Morals*. But when Nietzsche treats the will to power as the one big idea that explains everything, he risks going too far and rendering the concept unusable. For if all action is will to power – as the formulation 'Life as such is will to power' suggests – then there is no action that is *not* will to power, and explanations in terms of will to power become tautological.

Alternatively, we may conceive the will to power as animating or motivating action. In that case, however, we can observe its effects, but we cannot detect the will to power itself. It is either an unfalsifiable hypothesis, or, as some commentators have thought, a metaphysical idea that is concealed behind phenomena and can only be known *a priori*.[35] Yet Nietzsche has long insisted that metaphysical ideas are illusory, mere descendants of religious belief in another world. Perhaps it is not so easy to get rid of metaphysics after all.

Nietzsche as Poet

To criticize the intellectual framework of *Zarathustra* may be unfair, even irrelevant. It is not presented as a work of philosophy, but as a prose poem, containing not arguments but exhortations and prophecies. It recalls the prophetic books of the Old Testament, Jesus' discourses in the Gospels and speeches attributed to the Buddha.[36] Nietzsche noted in 1884: 'The language of Luther and the poetic form of the Bible as the basis of a new German *poetry* – that is *my* invention!' (*KSA* XI 60). Its most immediate model appears to have been the allegorical and mythological epic *Prometheus Unbound* (1876) by Siegfried Lipiner (1856–1911), which had in turn been influenced by *The Birth of Tragedy*.[37] Nietzsche so admired it that he wrote Lipiner a fan letter (24 August 1877). In *Zarathustra* one can also pick up distant echoes of Goethe, Hölderlin and Shelley.

Appropriately, *Zarathustra* appealed not only to the many readers who found Nietzsche's aphorisms too difficult, but to poets and composers. Richard Strauss's tone-poem *Also sprach Zarathustra* (1896) is only the best known of numerous compositions inspired by Nietzsche's text. The imagery of mountains, sky and sun encouraged many poets to write visionary epics, now largely (and perhaps unjustly) forgotten.[38] The Expressionist architect Bruno Taut sought to convert Zarathustra's landscape into an 'Alpine architecture' of glass domes and palaces.[39]

More recent readers have been less enthusiastic. The reputation of *Zarathustra* has admittedly not been helped by its appropriation for militarism in the First World War: some 150,000 soldiers carried *Zarathustra*, in a special wartime edition, with them to the front.[40] Above all, however, Nietzsche's prophetic prose has not worn well. Many modern readers have found it strained. J. P. Stern says that it arouses 'the sort of embarrassment one feels when faced with D. H. Lawrence at his "prophetic" worst'.[41]

Still, a less global, more differentiated judgement is possible. Many of Zarathustra's utterances are striking and memorable, and many passages have a rich lyrical beauty that loses much in translation: for example, the opening of the 'Night-Song', which Nietzsche singles out for self-praise (*EH* 'Z' 6):

Nacht ist es: nun reden lauter alle springenden Brunnen.
Und auch meine Seele ist ein springender Brunnen.
Nacht ist es: nun erst erwachen alle Lieder der Liebenden.
Und auch meine Seele ist das Lied eines Liebenden.

(Night it is: now all springing fountains talk more
loudly. And my soul too is a springing fountain.
Night it is: now all songs of lovers at last awaken.
And my soul too is the song of a lover. (*Z* II 9))

The difficulty is that lyrical intensity cannot be sustained throughout a long work. The bulk needs to be written in a calmer language to set off the lyrical flights. Nietzsche tries to sustain the rhetorical afflatus for too long, and too much of the text feels repetitive and tedious. Some of the passages that work best are those where Zarathustra's message is anchored to concrete images (as with the two long lanes and the spider crawling in the moonlight, III 2), or where he uses allegorical images that speak for themselves (as in 'On the Three Transformations', I 1). Despite his injunction to 'stay true to the earth', there is remarkably little of the earth in *Zarathustra*. The world evoked by the text is largely abstract, and hence Zarathustra's rhetoric is obliged to carry a weight that often makes it sound forced.

Nietzsche also wrote numerous shorter poems that deserve attention. *The Gay Science* opens with a group of verse epigrams headed 'Jest, Ruse and Revenge' (the title of an opera libretto by Goethe) and ends with 'Songs of Prince Free-as-a-Bird', a term connoting not only freedom but outlawry. The latter recycle several of the poems originally published in 1882 as 'Idylls from Messina'. *Beyond Good and Evil* ends with a poem entitled 'From High Mountains'. *Zarathustra* and *Ecce Homo* also contain verse passages. Immediately before his collapse in January 1889 Nietzsche made a fair copy of 'Dionysus Dithyrambs'. Other poems can be found in his notebooks.

Nietzsche skilfully employs a range of verse-forms, genres and poetic personae. He owes relatively little to the Romantic lyric, although the sequence headed 'The Free Spirit' ('Der Freigeist', not necessarily synonymous with Nietzsche's usual term 'der freie Geist') features a Romantic-sounding wanderer and wintry setting reminiscent of Wilhelm Müller's (and Franz Schubert's) *Winterreise* (KSA XI 329–32). The verse epigrams recall Goethe's, although Nietzsche's tone is more bitter and biting. Many of his poems are tinged with satire. Some, especially the 'Dithyrambs', are in free verse, markedly recalling the hymnic poetry of Klopstock, Hölderlin and the young Goethe. One of the poetic masks Nietzsche favours is Yorick, the jester whose skull Hamlet contemplates, implying that in the eyes of the world the prophet is merely a foolish poet. Another is Columbus, the seafarer who was in Nietzsche's mind whenever he visited Columbus' birthplace, Genoa, and who is often associated with Nietzsche's frequent image of voyages of discovery into unknown seas (GS 289, 291).

A few of Nietzsche's poems have shown themselves to be memorable and quotable. The poem headed 'The Desert Is Spreading' ('Die Wüste wächst', Z IV 16 and 'Dithyrambs' 2–3), was cited in his diary by the exiled Thomas Mann to express the devastation of German culture by enforced emigration, imprisonment and suicide. Among the epigrams in *The Gay Science*, one entitled 'Ecce Homo' stands out by its serious tone and poetic concentration:

> Ja! Ich weiss, woher ich stamme!
> Ungesättigt gleich der Flamme
> Glühe und verzehr' ich mich.
> Licht wird Alles, was ich fasse,
> Kohle Alles, was ich lasse:
> Flamme bin ich sicherlich. (GS 'Scherz' 62)

> (Yes! I know whence I descend!
> Unsatisfied like the flame,
> I glow and consume myself.
> All I grasp turns to light,
> all I leave to charcoal;
> I surely am a flame.)

The message here is ambivalent: the speaker's brilliance and passion consume his substance. Although the artistry of Nietzsche's verse is rarely comparable to that of his prose, his poems are not negligible as part of his oeuvre.

5

The Philosopher with the Hammer

During the 1880s we have many glimpses of Nietzsche from other visitors to Nice and Sils Maria. Although he was well known to be a scholar, people thought he looked more like a military man or a country squire. Adolf Ruthardt (1849–1934), a musician from Geneva who met him in 1885, left the following description:

> Nietzsche's external appearance made an extremely agreeable impression on me. Above middle height, slender, well-formed, with erect but not stiff stance, his gestures harmonious, calm and sparing; the almost black hair, the thick Vercingetorix mustache, his light-colored, but distinguished-looking suit of the best cut and fit, allowed him so little to resemble the type of a German scholar that he called to mind rather a Southern French nobleman or an Italian or Spanish higher officer in civilian clothes. Deep seriousness, but by no means the somber, angular, demonic expression that has been attributed to him in pictures and busts, spoke out of his noble features, with a healthy tan from going out a great deal in the open air and sun, and out of his large dark eyes.[1]

Although Nietzsche was not sociable, all reminiscences emphasize his courtesy and charm. He did not seem at all eccentric, unless when confiding the secret of the eternal recurrence. 'Nietzsche always was of the most perfect "gentilezza",' recalled Helen

Zimmern, an Englishwoman of German Jewish extraction who would later produce the first English version of *Beyond Good and Evil*.[2] He got on well with ladies both young and old. Meta von Salis and her female companion taught him how to row a boat. He was fond of an elderly Catholic Irishwoman, Emily Fynn, and begged her with tears in his eyes not to read his books, as they would only make her unhappy.[3] A Russian lady, Madame de Mansuroff, suffered a mental disturbance and refused to leave her room, although her friends were waiting with a carriage to transport her to a more congenial climate in Italy; Nietzsche intervened and presently reappeared with the old lady following him obediently.[4]

Although Nietzsche had many spells of relatively good health, he still suffered intermittently from crippling headaches. He worried a lot about his diet. At one time, according to the hotel-keeper in Sils Maria, he lived mainly on fruit, sometimes eating almost 3 kilograms a day. Later he decided that a vegetarian diet was bad for him and ate mainly meat and eggs, despite his difficulty in digesting them. He does not seem to have been in regular contact with a doctor, thinking that he understood his physical condition and its treatment better than any physician. So, as Resa von Schirnhofer reports, in Rapallo in 1882 he composed prescriptions for himself, signed them 'Dr Nietzsche' as though he were a medical doctor and had them prepared by unsuspecting chemists.[5] He took long walks, usually carrying a parasol to keep off the sun.

Insomnia was a problem. Nietzsche's mind was constantly racing. In 1884, looking exhausted, he said to Schirnhofer, 'I never get any rest,' and asked her whether she thought this condition was a prelude to madness, as his father had died of a brain disease.[6] To help him sleep, he took chloral hydrate, a drug often used in the late nineteenth century as a sedative, although nowadays it is not approved for medical use; it may have done him more harm than good.

The feverish intellectual excitement in which Nietzsche lived is apparent not only from the books he produced during this period

– *Beyond Good and Evil* (1886), *The Genealogy of Morals* (1887), *The Case of Wagner* (1888) and *Twilight of the Idols* (1889), besides *The Antichrist* and *Ecce Homo*, which were published posthumously in 1895 and 1908 respectively – but from his extensive notes. It was from these that Köselitz and others, strictly directed by Elisabeth Nietzsche, would compile *The Will to Power*.

Despite his failing eyesight, Nietzsche also read intensively, making marginal notes. When he had to borrow a book from a library, he often copied out extracts into his notebooks. Hence it is now possible to reconstruct his intellectual life in considerable detail, using not only his notebooks but his personal library, preserved in the Nietzsche Archive at Weimar.

Much of Nietzsche's reading in the early 1880s was philosophical and scientific.[7] His approach to his reading was combative, reminiscent of the Greek *agon*. He read antagonistic thinkers in order to argue against them and reinforce his own beliefs. Thus, to strengthen his rejection of pessimism, he returned to pessimistic philosophers such as Schopenhauer and Philipp Mainländer (1841–1876). Mainländer argued in *The Philosophy of Redemption* (1876) that all living beings were really striving for non-existence. He practised his philosophy: the day he received a copy of his great work, he committed suicide on the grounds that his life no longer had any purpose.[8]

With science, Nietzsche combatted some of the prevailing assumptions of the time. The approach labelled positivism denied any metaphysical entities and claimed that all knowledge was derived from the senses and could only be verified by scientific and logical investigation. Nietzsche agreed in rejecting metaphysics (or trying to do so), but did not think knowledge was so easily accessible. He argued instead that there is no pure or unmediated experience, and that experience is always the result of interpretation. Here he found himself in agreement with such philosophers of science as Ernst Mach, for whom all knowledge is an abstraction from a flux of sensations: 'Knowledge is not the impossible notion of correspondence to a reality external to us but the stabilizing and reconciling of sensation in concepts and theories governed by the scientific criterion of economy. [. . .] Theories are tools serving the needs of life.'[9]

The final nail in the coffin of positivism, Nietzsche thought, had been driven in by the physicist Ruggero Boscovich, whom he had first read in 1873 and whom he repeatedly cited in the 1880s (mistakenly calling him a Pole, *BGE* 12, instead of a Croat). Positivist science presupposed materialism. Boscovich had shown that materialist atomism was untenable. What physicists called the 'impact' of one body on another could not occur; rather, an attractive force encountered a repulsive force. Matter consisted not of atoms but of extensionless points surrounded by fields of force. The solid bodies we think we perceive are an illusion, as is matter: 'Matter is nothing but the field of force which occupies the whole of space.'[10] 'Since [Boscovich], matter no longer exists,' wrote Nietzsche to Köselitz (20 March 1882). Copernicus had disproved our illusion that the sun goes round the earth; Boscovich followed him by disproving matter, and thus confirming that our apparent experience is deceptive – 'the greatest triumph over the senses that has ever been gained on earth' (*BGE* 12).

Later in the decade Nietzsche took a new, highly critical interest in religion. In 1885 he read St Augustine's *Confessions* and laughed at the dishonesty of the 'old rhetorician' (to Overbeck, 31 March 1885). He went on to read Renan's *Life of Jesus*, Tolstoy's *What I Believe* (which maintains that the core of Jesus' teaching, 'Resist not him that is evil,' has been consistently falsified by the Churches) and the epoch-making studies of the Old Testament by Julius Wellhausen (1844–1918). Wellhausen reversed the accepted chronology of the religious development of ancient Israel, showing that the Law had not been proclaimed by Moses in the wilderness but had been composed at a later date by priests who wrote down a false version of history. In August 1888 Nietzsche also had many conversations with another visitor to Sils Maria, the theologian Julius Kaftan (1848–1926), an old acquaintance from Basel. Immediately after Kaftan's departure, Nietzsche began writing *Der Antichrist* (the title means both 'Antichrist', God's antagonist, and 'anti-Christian'), which draws extensively on the notes he had taken from Wellhausen and delivers a furious polemic against priestly Judaism and its successor, Christianity, for destroying classical culture and enfeebling modern Europe.

From at least 1884 to September 1888, Nietzsche worked intermittently on a magnum opus which was to offer a philosophy for the future. Various titles, plans and content summaries can be followed through his notebooks and letters. In summer 1884 its working title is *Philosophy of Eternal Recurrence: An Attempt at the Revaluation of All Values*. In August 1885 we find the title *The Will to Power: An Attempt at a New Interpretation of Everything that Happens*, changed by summer 1886 to *The Will to Power: An Attempt at a Revaluation of All Values*. It was this title that his posthumous editors, Elisabeth Förster-Nietzsche and Heinrich Köselitz, chose for their compilation from his notebooks, along with one of the various four-part plans Nietzsche sketched. That plan had been discarded by 26 August 1888, when Nietzsche for the last time uses *The Will to Power* as a book title, adding a quite different and very elaborate scheme of chapters (*KSA* XIII 537–8). Another notebook entry, from September 1888, uses *Revaluation of all Values* as the main title, with yet another four-part scheme, the first section being entitled 'The Antichrist' (*KSA* XIII 545). On 26 November he told Deussen: 'My Revaluation of All Values, with its main title The Antichrist, is complete.' Evidently he had now discarded the whole idea of a magnum opus.

Instead, he rapidly produced several shorter works. One was a selection from his notebooks intended as a digest of his philosophy, originally entitled *Idle Hours of a Psychologist* and later published as *Twilight of the Idols* (completed by late September 1888). A polemical analysis of Wagner's work, *The Case of Wagner*, completed in August 1888, provided 'light relief' (to Meysenbug, 4 October 1888). Another short work was his autobiography, *Ecce Homo*, written within a month (15 October–14 November 1888). Like *The Antichrist*, it appeared only after Nietzsche's collapse. Nietzsche wrote to Meysenbug that *The Antichrist* was 'the greatest philosophical event of all time, with which the history of mankind falls into two halves' (4 October 1888).

With such tremendous thoughts running through his head, and engaged feverishly in writing and revising, it is no wonder that Nietzsche often struck other people as distant and unapproachable. When he and Rohde met for the last time, in 1888, Rohde felt upset by Nietzsche's remoteness: 'as though he came from a country where nobody else lived'.[11]

However, particularly in the later 1880s, Nietzsche read widely in literature and discussed it with his holiday acquaintances. He preferred to ignore German literature, apart from such favourites as Eckermann's *Conversations with Goethe*, Stifter's *Der Nachsommer* and Keller's *Der grüne Heinrich*. He was enthusiastic about French literature, and although he spoke French badly, he evidently had little difficulty in understanding it when read aloud or in reading it, with the occasional help of a dictionary. A favourite was Stendhal, of whom his friend Paul Lanzky read three volumes aloud to him in Nice in 1884; he gave Resa von Schirnhofer a copy of *The Red and the Black*.[12] He admired Baudelaire, despite considering him 'three-quarters mad' (to Köselitz, 26 February 1888), and a host of others. Although he mentions Flaubert and Zola a few times, it is not clear whether he ever actually read them.

A great discovery, made in 1887, was Dostoevsky, read in French translation. 'Do you know Dostoevsky?' he asked Köselitz (13 February 1887): 'Apart from Stendhal, nobody has given me so much pleasure and surprise: a psychologist "I can get on with".'

Nietzsche first read *Notes from Underground* and went on to other works, seeming particularly struck by *The Insulted and Injured* (where the amoral credo of Prince Valkonsky must have appealed to him). Curiously, his letters do not mention any of the four great novels conventionally considered central to Dostoevsky's oeuvre, although his notebooks show familiarity with *The Devils* (*KSA* XIII 142–50). Another very late discovery, made in 1888, was Strindberg, with whom Nietzsche corresponded. He read *The Father*, Strindberg's powerful drama of misogyny, twice, reporting to his Sils Maria friend Emily Fynn that 'it is said to have shattered even Zola's nerves' (6 December 1888).

Aside from holiday acquaintances, Nietzsche's personal relationships tended to dwindle. Despite their estrangement, he was deeply saddened by the news of Wagner's death on 13 February 1883. 'I loved and revered Richard Wagner more than I did anybody else,' he wrote in his notebook (*KSA* XII 80). But he continued to deplore Wagner's decline into nationalism and religiosity. Fortunately Nietzsche found a new composer to admire: Georges Bizet. He heard Bizet's opera *Carmen* (1875) for the first time in Genoa on 27 November 1881, and thereafter attended every performance he could. In contrast to German heaviness, Bizet represented for him the artistic spirit and psychological subtlety that seemed characteristic of France and redolent of the Mediterranean – music for 'good Europeans': 'It is for them that *Bizet* made music, that last genius to perceive a new beauty and a new seduction – who has discovered a region of the *south in music*' (*BGE* 254).[13]

Nietzsche's relations with his sister Elisabeth were strained, sometimes hostile. He was angry with her, not only because she had intervened in the Lou affair, but because she was increasingly involved in the growing antisemitic movement. Nietzsche detested antisemitism. He deplored it in Wagner, and he himself shows no sign of it: although he broke with Rée, he never held Rée's Jewish ancestry against him, and he admired the Jewish poets Heine and Lipiner. Writing to the latter, Nietzsche hoped he was a Jew, 'because I have recently had many experiences that give me *very great* expectations from young men of this background' (24 August 1877). Unfortunately, as Nietzsche reported with disgust, Lipiner later converted to Christianity and himself became an antisemite (to Overbeck, 7 April 1884).

During her stay in Bayreuth in 1882, Elisabeth met Dr Bernhard Förster, a prominent antisemite who had plans to found a colony of pure-blooded Germans in South America. He spent from 1883 to 1885 travelling in search of a suitable location and thought he had found it in Paraguay, where a colony could be established using the natives as a labour force. On his return to Europe, he married Elisabeth; Nietzsche did not attend, but sent them a copy of Dürer's engraving *Knight, Death and the Devil* as a present. The one time he met Förster, in October 1885, Nietzsche found his brother-in-law 'not unsympathetic', but a vigorous man of action who took decisions with too little thought (to Overbeck, 17 October 1885).

This proved an accurate assessment. Förster and Elisabeth sailed for Paraguay in February 1886 with a party of hopeful colonists. The colony never prospered: its land was infertile, the markets for its meagre produce were too remote. A critical traveller reported that the Försters lived in comfort, the other colonists in miserable shacks, and that the courageous and resolute Elisabeth completely dominated her husband. Finally Förster absconded with the colony's funds, went on a drinking spree in Asunción (the Paraguayan capital) and shot himself.[14]

Nietzsche also had difficult relations with his publishers. His original publisher, Fritzsch, became insolvent in 1874 and had to give up his business. Another publisher, Ernst Schmeitzner, made Nietzsche an offer which he accepted. Schmeitzner was a poor businessman, and, even more to Nietzsche's discomfort, he was an antisemite who issued a prominent antisemitic journal,

Elisabeth Förster-
Nietzsche, 1894.

so that Nietzsche risked seeming to be linked with beliefs he
hated. Nevertheless, when Schmeitzner's business was struggling,
Nietzsche made him several loans and it took a lawsuit to get them
repaid. Nietzsche returned to Fritzsch but was obliged to pay the
publication costs of his subsequent books. All this, besides the
worry it cost him, confirmed his sense of isolation. *Zarathustra*,
conceived as a 'Fifth Gospel' (to Schmeitzner, 13 February 1883), had
sold hardly any copies. 'Enduring these last years was perhaps the
hardest thing my fate has imposed on me,' he wrote to Overbeck
(17 June 1887). 'After such an appeal from the inmost soul as my
Zarathustra was, to hear not a sound in reply, nothing, nothing,
always only the silent loneliness, now increased a thousandfold –
that has something inconceivably dreadful about it, the strongest
person might perish from it – alas, and I am not "the strongest"!'

Hence Nietzsche's overwhelming joy when he learned that the internationally distinguished Danish literary critic Georg Brandes, to whom he had sent copies of *Beyond Good and Evil* and *The Genealogy of Morals*, was lecturing on his work to large audiences in Copenhagen. Brandes was not a wholly uncritical admirer: he demurred at the lack of nuance in Nietzsche's arguments and regretted the over-hasty dismissal of socialism. He described Nietzsche's standpoint as 'aristocratic radicalism', a term which Nietzsche was delighted to accept as 'the cleverest thing I have ever read about myself' (to Brandes, 2 December 1887).

So Nietzsche was entitled to hope that his painful obscurity was approaching an end. But, although one must be cautious about detecting foreshadowings of his later collapse, he was undeniably showing signs of eccentricity. In the curriculum vitae he sent Brandes, he asserted that he was descended from Polish nobles called Niezky (to Brandes, 10 April 1888). He had nourished this entirely baseless fantasy for some years, confiding it to Resa von Schirnhofer in 1884.[15] He also told his friends darkly about the prodigious task he had undertaken: 'I want to force humanity to take decisions that will determine the entire human future, and it may well be that entire millennia will make their highest vows in my name' (to Meysenbug, early June 1884; similarly to Overbeck, 21 May 1884, and to Heinrich von Stein, 22 May 1884). Such boasts, which one is tempted to call megalomaniac, fill his autobiography, *Ecce Homo*, written in autumn 1888 but not published (and then, thanks to Elisabeth's interventions, with large omissions) until 1908. Here the Polish fantasy recurs in heightened form: 'I am a pure-blooded Polish nobleman without a drop of inferior blood, least of all German' (*EH* 'Wise' 3). So does the self-aggrandizement, especially in the final section headed 'Why I am a Destiny': 'One day my name will be linked with the memory of something monstrous – a crisis such as there has never been on earth' (*EH* 'Destiny' 1).

In 1888 Nietzsche decided to try out an Italian city new to him. On 5 April he arrived in Turin and fell in love with it.[16] In ecstatic letters he praised its well-preserved seventeenth-century architecture, its arcades giving shelter from the sun, its climate, its food, its three foreign-language bookshops and the pleasing coincidence that *Carmen* was being performed in its opera house (to Köselitz, 7 April 1888). After the misery recorded in so many previous letters, the reader is naturally glad to find Nietzsche happy. But his euphoria seems tinged with narcissism: 'The remarkable thing about Turin is the complete fascination I exert, although I am the most modest of men and demand *nothing*. But when I enter a large shop, every face changes; the women in the street look at me, – my old fruit-seller puts the sweetest grapes aside for me and *lowers the price*!' (to Overbeck, Christmas 1888). He is clearly over-compensating for his isolation. Meanwhile, when not strolling round Turin, he was writing furiously. In his texts, especially *Ecce Homo*, over-compensation often became megalomania; likewise when he wrote to Overbeck that he intended

Panoramic view of Turin, 1890s.

Bust of Nietzsche on the ground floor of Villa Silberblick, Weimar, which now houses the Nietzsche Archive.

to found an anti-German league and provoke the empire into war (26 December 1888). His notebooks for the same month contain fantasies about 'great politics' and waging war on the Hohenzollern dynasty (KSA XIII 637, 643).

Early in January 1889 Nietzsche fired off incoherent letters, not only to many acquaintances, but to the king of Italy and Cardinal Mariani. A long letter to Burckhardt (dated 6 January 1889, but probably written earlier) ended with the paragraph 'I have had Caiaphas chained up; also last year I was crucified very slowly by the German doctors. Wilhelm[,] Bismarck and all antisemites abolished.' Burckhardt consulted Overbeck, who had also received a mad letter, signed 'Dionysos' (4 January 1889). Overbeck travelled overnight to Turin, arriving in the afternoon of 8 January, and found Nietzsche reading on a sofa; Nietzsche rushed up to him and embraced him in a flood of tears, then fell back on the sofa, twitching all over.[17] In the meantime, perhaps on the 3rd but more likely on the 7th, Nietzsche had collapsed in the street. A dubious

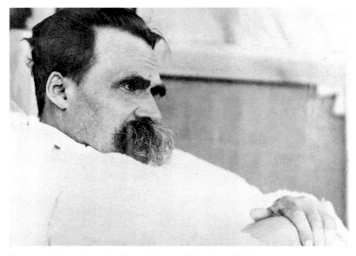

Photograph from the series *Nietzsche the Invalid* by Hans Olde, between June and August 1889.

story, not found in print before 1930, says that he embraced a cab-horse that was being beaten by its driver. This, however, would be uncharacteristic of Nietzsche, who never shows concern for animals; if it did happen, he may have been trying to save himself from falling. With some difficulty, Overbeck induced Nietzsche to accompany him to Basel and enter a psychiatric clinic. On 17 January he was transferred to a clinic in Jena so that his mother could visit him regularly, and in May they both moved to her house in Naumburg. Thereafter Franziska Nietzsche tended her son devotedly. He showed little understanding of what was happening, but behaved mostly with childlike docility.

Elisabeth, who returned from Paraguay in September 1893, found that Nietzsche's books were now in such demand that his publisher, Naumann, was issuing his collected works. She established the Nietzsche Archive, initially in her mother's house in Naumburg, then, after Franziska Nietzsche's death on 20 April 1896,

Edvard Munch, *Friedrich Nietzsche*, 1906, oil on canvas.

in its present location, the Villa Silberblick, then on the outskirts of Weimar, where Elisabeth also lived with her brother. Visitors found it impossible to communicate with Nietzsche. Resa von Schirnhofer recalls her visit in autumn 1897:

> Nietzsche, much heavier than formerly, had the typical appearance of an older, quietly satisfied man, fixed in a state

Edvard Munch, *Elisabeth Förster-Nietzsche*, 1906, oil on canvas.

of rest. I stood at the door while Frau Elisabeth, nodding to her brother, said: 'Look, Fritz, the person coming in the door is Resa Schirnhofer.' But the peacefully sitting heavy figure did not raise his somewhat bowed head, did not look over, and gave no sign that Nietzsche had even heard his sister's remark. Immobile, apathetic, sealed off in a world of his own, he sat there like a robot where someone else's will had set him. I do not remember saying a word of greeting and overcoming the anxious stiffness that seized me at the sight of this personality whom I had once known and who was now so unknown and silent. I only know that his sister said he was not having a good day that day. So I left sadly, pondering what thoughts and feelings might still be alive behind that impenetrable external mask in this form of life which bore the seal of human helplessness and in which every spark of mental life seemed extinguished.[18]

After a succession of strokes, Nietzsche died on 25 August 1900.

Life versus Philosophy

Nietzsche's later works, despite or because of his own isolation, are explicitly addressed to an imagined community of 'free spirits'. The character of the free spirit, already sketched in *Human, All-Too-Human*, is now developed further. Free spirits are entirely different from the democratic and liberal 'freethinkers' of modern Europe (*BGE* 44). Instead of repeating *bien-pensant* platitudes, free spirits are committed to 'honesty' (*Redlichkeit*, *BGE* 227), to independence of all personal, national or intellectual ties that might limit their thought (*BGE* 41), to questioning all assumptions, whatever danger zones their questioning may lead to. They are strong enough that they no longer need beliefs or convictions; firm beliefs are always a sign of weakness (*GS* 347). Instead, they are experimental thinkers (*BGE* 42). Nietzsche quotes from Stendhal, 'the last great psychologist', the view that for discoveries in philosophy, 'for seeing clearly into that which is', one needs the same qualities as a successful banker: one must be 'dry, clear, without illusion' (*BGE* 39).

It is free spirits who can carry out Nietzsche's much-quoted injunction 'Become who you are!' He contrasts them with the vast majority of people who are prisoners of the past: 'We, however, *want to become those we are* – the new, the unique, the incomparable, those who give themselves laws, those who create themselves!' But for that, Nietzsche continues, the free spirits must understand the material conditions governing their existence, right down to the laws of physics. Hence he concludes: 'Long live physics! And even longer that which compels us to study physics – our honesty [*Redlichkeit*]!' (*GS* 335).[19]

So free spirits seek the truth. Yet the preface to *Beyond Good and Evil* warns that truth is elusive; its first sentence asserts that truth is a woman, and suggests that philosophers so far have been clumsy wooers. Philosophy has usually been an attempt by philosophers to construct another world that lies outside life and provides the basis for a philosophical explanation of this world. Plato appealed to an unchanging realm of Ideas. Kant called reality the *Ding an sich*; it was inaccessible because the only world we can understand is the one made possible by our intellectual and perceptual apparatus, which obliges us to experience the world in terms of time, space and causality. Other philosophers have made bold claims about reality, which Nietzsche seeks to debunk. Idealists claim that the external world is created by our organs of perception; but since our organs of perception are themselves part of the external world, this claim is self-contradictory (*BGE* 15). Descartes sought to ground philosophy on the supposedly self-evident proposition 'I think, therefore I am,' but this presupposes that one knows what 'I' means and what 'thinking' is.

Nietzsche puts forward many arguments against the supposed autonomy of philosophical thought. Thought is an instinctive process, helping to sustain life; philosophical thought is no different. Philosophers need to use language, and it may be that the structure of their language shapes their philosophy: thus the philosophical distinction between subject and object may just reflect the grammar of Indo-European languages.

In Nietzsche's opinion, the 'self' is yet another illusion. When we act, there is no separate 'I' directing our actions. If we think so, we are misled by the grammar of sentences which require every predicate to be preceded by a subject (*BGE* 17). A century earlier, the satirist Georg Christoph Lichtenberg, whose work Nietzsche knew well, had maintained that one should not say 'I think' but 'It is thinking,' as we say 'It is raining': 'To assume, to postulate an *I*, is a practical need.'[20] Nietzsche shares this scepticism, but goes further: 'there is no "being" behind doing, acting, becoming; "the doer" is merely a fiction imposed on the doing – the doing itself is everything' (*GM* I 13).[21]

If there is no actor, but only actions, how people act is not the result of a prior decision, but an expression of their natures. Hence there is no point in blaming strong, aggressive people for acting aggressively, any more than one can blame eagles for preying on lambs. The eagles follow their nature, just as a Caesar or a Napoleon follows his. Universal moral rules are therefore absurd: you cannot expect eagles to behave like lambs.[22]

Earlier, Nietzsche asserted that there was no such thing as freedom of the will. Now he rejects both the 'free will' and the 'unfree will' as imaginary notions, based on the fiction of 'cause' and 'effect'. All the concepts with which we make sense of the world – including number, reason, law, purpose – are equally fictions: mental constructions which we project onto the world as our mythology. 'The "unfree will" is mythology: real life is concerned only with *strong* or *weak* wills' (*BGE* 21). This is not the absolute determinism of *Human, All-Too-Human*, but the claim that people act and must act in accordance with their characters. A Homeric warrior could decide whether to spare or kill an enemy, but he was not free to ignore all concern for honour, because that would have been out of character.[23] Nietzsche often insists that one's actions, including the kind of philosophy one develops, proceed from one's character, which in turn is shaped by one's physical and physiological constitution.

Freedom therefore consists in the willing acceptance of necessity, including the acceptance of one's own character; Nietzsche calls this attitude 'amor fati' (love of fate): 'I wish to learn more and more to see the necessity in things as beauty: – thus I shall be one of those who make things beautiful. *Amor fati*: let that be my love henceforth!' (GS 276; cf. EH 'Clever' 10, CW 4).[24] He broadly agrees with Spinoza's doctrine that freedom is the knowledge of necessity.[25] The erroneous idea of free will can be explained genetically: the weak wanted someone to blame for their sufferings, so invented the idea that the strong were not just following their natures but *freely chose* to oppress them (GM I 13).

Moral concepts such as 'good' and 'evil' are also fictional. Antitheses do not exist in reality, only in the constructions of philosophers. Preachers of morality condemn bad passions such as hatred, envy, greed and the like. But these have a necessary place in the economy of life (BGE 23). They help to provide the energy that sustains and heightens life. We cannot do without them, however shocking moralizers may find this discovery. Thus Nietzsche's picture of the world is 'beyond good and evil'.

At the outset, Nietzsche challenges the very conception of the philosophical search for truth. Why do we want truth in the first place? Where does the so-called 'will to truth' come from? Are there not many falsehoods and errors which are more valuable, because they are more life-enhancing and life-sustaining, than truths? 'The falseness of a judgement is to us not necessarily an objection to a judgement: it is here that our new language perhaps sounds strangest. The question is to what extent it is life-advancing, life-preserving, species-preserving, perhaps even species-breeding' (*bge* 4).

Not only have philosophers supposed truth to be a timeless metaphysical reality, they have often put forward concepts that on examination prove tautological or vacuous. The Stoics, for example, advocated living according to nature; but as we are natural beings, that is the only way we *can* live (*bge* 9). Most philosophers have simply elaborated their prejudices into an intellectual system. They may think they are above the battle, quietly contemplating the universe, but they too are animated by the will to power, which makes them strive to impose their world-picture not only on their fellow thinkers but on the world itself. Philosophy reveals little about the world, but much about philosophers. All philosophy is disguised autobiography (*bge* 6).

Opposing late nineteenth-century positivism, Nietzsche denies that natural science has any claim to absolute truth. Physics does not offer us an eternally valid explanation of the world; it only offers an interpretation. Positivist science expresses the democratic prejudices of nineteenth-century scientists: in claiming that nature is governed by invariable laws, they are just transposing onto nature the democratic ideal of equality before the law. 'Scientific law' is only a metaphor, like other concepts used in interpreting the world. 'Cause' and 'effect' are only conventional fictions imposed on reality:

In the 'in itself' there is nothing of 'causal connection', of 'necessity', of 'psychological unfreedom'; there 'the effect' *does not* 'follow the cause', there no 'law' rules. It is *we* alone who have fabricated causes, succession, reciprocity, relativity, compulsion, number, law, freedom, motive, purpose; and when we falsely introduce this world of symbols into things and mingle it with them as though this symbol-world were an 'in itself', we once more behave as we have always behaved, namely *mythologically*. (*bge* 21)

The cosmos presented by modern science, therefore, is just another mythology. Granted, it works; it enables us to operate with nature. But that does not mean that it can claim absolute truth. It does not possess the metaphysical authority, the timeless verity, to which philosophers aspire.

Does Nietzsche actually maintain, as some recent admirers have claimed, that there is no such thing as truth? He comes close to it when he suggests that the anti-idealists and anti-metaphysicians who are guided by their intellectual conscience are actually mistaken: 'These men are far from *free* spirits: *for they still believe in the truth!*' (*GM* III 24). Nietzsche then tells us about the Assassins, an oriental 'order of free spirits *par excellence*', who guarded the secret that 'Nothing is true, everything is permitted.'[26] This story seems to say not only that there are no moral sanctions ('everything is permitted') but that there is no truth on which such sanctions could be based. It opens up the dizzying possibility that one might shape the world according to one's will, or, like 'new Nietzscheans', engage in 'the joyous affirmation of the play of the world and the innocence of becoming, the affirmation of a world of signs without fault, without truth'.[27] However, it leads to the same contradiction as all extreme scepticism, for the Assassins were implicitly saying, 'It is true that nothing is true.' So Nietzsche rows back to asking about the value of truth, and thereby presupposes that truth exists.

Nietzsche uses the word 'truth' in different ways. Sometimes he means absolute truth: certain knowledge about how the world really is in itself; such truth is unattainable, because we live in a world shaped by our sense-organs and mental capacities, and cannot get outside our world to compare it with the 'real' world. Absolute truth is one of the metaphysical chimeras that Nietzsche is combating. But he is easily led into rhetorical flights where he declares that there is *no* truth of any kind: 'we free spirits [. . .] are an *incarnate* declaration of war and victory over all ancient conceptions of "true" and "false"' (*A* 13).

Sometimes, however, Nietzsche means the common-sense notion of truth as knowledge about *our* world, obtained by careful scrutiny and scrupulous reasoning. He does not deny that it is possible to attain such truth. His historical investigations, *The Genealogy of Morals* and *The Antichrist*, are extended enquiries into truth, however unpleasant such truth must be: 'the service of truth is the hardest service' (*A* 50). He considers it valuable to expose falsehood by discovering the truth. In *The Antichrist* he opposes the lies of Christianity by appealing to the 'reality' discovered by 'the two great opponents of all superstition: philology and medicine' (*A* 47). His vehement attacks on priestly lies would be meaningless if he were not countering them with the truth.

Yet it is not obvious to Nietzsche why anyone should struggle to attain truth. It is not pleasant, after all, to learn that the self is an illusion, that all life ends in extinction, that there is no loving God to console people for their suffering. Many falsehoods are not only pleasant but beneficial. The search for truth may be motivated by a wish not to be deceived, and thus be prudential; but since some falsehoods are useful, and some truths may even be destructive, it is not clear why one should always prefer truth. The will to truth must therefore not be prudential, but moral, resting 'on the ground of morality' (*GS* 344). That raises the question of the origin of morality, which Nietzsche pursues in *The Genealogy of Morals*.

Two obstacles to finding truth, often mentioned in Nietzsche's later writings, are the concepts of 'perspective' and 'interpretation'. Nietzsche is sometimes credited with putting forward a doctrine called 'perspectivism', although he uses this term only once (*GS* 354). He explains that the nature of our consciousness, which we share with animals, means that we only ever perceive a selective and simplified version of the world, in which particulars are translated into general signs.[28] Hence in *The Genealogy of Morals* Nietzsche challenges standard notions of scientific objectivity. They are just as absurd as Kant's concept of 'disinterested pleasure'. 'Perspectival seeing is the *only* kind of seeing there is, perspectival "knowing" the only kind of "knowing"' (*GM* III 13).

In saying that all knowledge is from a perspective, Nietzsche is sometimes thought to be claiming that all knowledge is equally false.[29] If so, he would fall foul of the Cretan liar paradox ('All Cretans are liars, said Epimenides the Cretan'). If all knowledge is from a perspective, that statement must itself come from a perspective and imply the existence of another perspective from which *not* all knowledge is perspectival. Some of Nietzsche's commentators have laboured to save him from self-contradiction, pointing out that perspectival knowledge is not necessarily false, just incomplete.[30] Nietzsche himself says that for a better view of any matter, we need to assemble a variety of perspectives: 'the *more* eyes, different eyes through which we are able to view this same matter, the more complete our "conception" of it, our "objectivity", will be' (*GM* III 12).[31] In any case, not all perspectives are equally valid: the perspective of the unsophisticated observer who thinks the earth is flat is clearly inferior to the perspective of the scientist who knows that it is spherical.[32]

Nietzsche may again appear to profess total scepticism when he asserts that even scientific knowledge is only an interpretation of the world, guided by metaphors. When nature is said to be subject to invariable laws, physicists are really projecting onto nature the values of modern democracy, where all are equal before the law. Nature could be described by another set of metaphors, in which (to develop Nietzsche's argument a little) gravitation and magnetism could be described as expressions of a will to power, so that the magnet commands iron filings to approach it (*BGE* 22).

Such claims are daring, but not senseless. An analogy with literary interpretation may be helpful. Few people now suppose that an interpreter can give a complete interpretation of any text, nor one wholly independent of the interpreter's time and circumstances. If we follow Nietzsche in treating the world as a text, there may be innumerable interpretations, some much better than others, none complete or timeless, none able to claim absolute authority. Like the literary text, the world as text is inaccessible except via interpretations, but it is not created by interpreters. Similarly, we have various incomplete perspectives on reality, but reality is not brought into being by our perspectives.

Nietzsche condemns previous philosophers, not for thinking that truth is possible, but for over-confidently claiming to possess it. Instead of dogmatic assertion, he advocates open enquiry, thought-experiments, speculations. Future thinkers will be 'philosophers of the dangerous Perhaps' (*BGE* 2), *Versucher* (implying both 'experimenters' and 'tempters', *BGE* 42).

Homo natura

Turning to morality, Nietzsche puts forward a 'natural history of morals'. With this phrase, he evokes a long tradition of Enlightenment thinking that sought to trace humanity's moral and religious sentiments back not to supernatural but to natural origins.[33] Nietzsche continues this tradition by his thorough-going naturalism, that is, his understanding of humanity as entirely a part of nature.[34] Nietzsche proposes 'to translate man back into nature; to master the many vain and fanciful interpretations and secondary meanings which have been hitherto scribbled and daubed over the eternal basic text *homo natura*' (*BGE* 230).

Man is an animal. But what kind of animal? Unlike other animals, man's nature is still developing: he is 'the animal *whose nature has not yet been fixed*' (*BGE* 62). That is why man very seldom attains the health of which he is capable. For the most part, man is '*the* sick animal', 'the most endangered, the most chronically and deeply sick of all the sick animals' (*GM* III 13). But his sickness, his estrangement from his animal instincts, also makes him rewarding to study: 'man is, relatively speaking, the most unsuccessful animal, the sickliest, the one most dangerously strayed from its instincts – with all that, to be sure, the most *interesting*!' (*A* 14). Humanity offers a fascinating field for analysis, and also, because human nature is still provisional, an object whose development needs to be directed. For the past two millennia humanity in Europe has been shaped, and damaged, by Christianity; Nietzsche hopes to indicate how the damage can be repaired and humanity pointed in a new direction, towards the fulfilment of its potential.

In the section of *Beyond Good and Evil* entitled 'On the Natural History of Morals', Nietzsche complains that philosophers have always taken their own morality for granted and sought to ground it theoretically, whereas they ought to have addressed morality itself as a problem. There is no one morality: across the world, and throughout history, there are and have been many different moralities. Nietzsche had already shown the vast difference between the morality of ancient Greece, which condoned slavery and genocide, and that of modern Europe. Moral conduct is generally founded not on reason, but on what Nietzsche earlier called *Sittlichkeit der Sitte*, the morality of custom. Custom has become so ingrained as to form a second nature, an instinct. The Athenians annoyed Socrates by acting on instinct, as all aristocrats do, and being unable to supply him with reasons for their conduct (*BGE* 191). The aristocrat, one might amplify, when asked for reasons, just replies 'Because'; the behaviour appropriate to his caste has been inculcated by tradition and convention. In Nietzsche's view, to ask '*Why* should I do this?' is plebeian; it presupposes that conduct has a utilitarian basis; and the question 'What purpose is served by my conduct?' easily leads to the vulgar, self-interested question 'What's in it for me?'

Morality often has an ignoble practical foundation. Many ostensibly moral precepts are pieces of prudent advice. This applies particularly to counsels of self-control. From the *apatheia* or insensibility recommended by the Stoics, down to the advocacy of moderation in all things, these counsels convey fear of the passions. Emotions must be restrained, because they will be dangerous if they get out of control (*BGE* 198). What the advocates of moderation most fear is the type of person Nietzsche calls the 'man of prey' (*Raubmensch*, analogous to *Raubtier*, 'beast of prey'), represented by unscrupulous Renaissance aristocrats such as Cesare Borgia. It was Borgia whom Machiavelli in 1513 praised in his amoral conduct manual for rulers, *The Prince*, advising that a ruler should combine the ruthlessness of a lion with the cunning of a fox. People like Borgia, according to Nietzsche, are 'tropical', like the luxuriant plants that flourish in tropical countries (*BGE* 197). They are not sick or secretly unhappy, as their pious detractors claim; rather, they are supremely healthy. But they are certainly dangerous.

The morality of fear goes back to the Jews, whose prophets lumped the words 'rich', 'godless', 'evil', 'violent' and 'sensual' together and denounced them all as attributes of 'the world' (*BGE* 195). They thus performed the extraordinary feat of rejecting the world (which, since nothing exists but the world, is tantamount to rejecting reality), and began what Nietzsche calls 'the slave revolt in morals' (*BGE* 195). The history of this revolt will be filled out in *The Genealogy of Morals*, but Nietzsche provides a foretaste by giving a potted history of European morals (*BGE* 199). Here he draws a crucial contrast between people who command and people who obey. The latter have always been the great majority. They internalize commands, such as the 'Thou shalt' with which the Ten Commandments begin, and obey the consciences that they have thus created. Eventually obedience becomes universal. Even those capable of command disguise their natures from themselves by claiming that in giving orders they are only obeying a higher authority (that of the constitution, the law or God). This is the state of affairs in present-day Europe: a few commanders, who dare not issue commands in their own name, amid a vast herd of the obedient, who identify morality only with those practices useful to the herd, such as benevolence, pity, moderation and industry.

The predominant morality in Europe is now herd morality, based on fear (*BGE* 201). Claiming to be the *only* morality, it preaches kindness, gentleness and humanitarianism, and condemns such dangerous urges as greed, cunning, risk-taking, vengefulness and the lust for power. The morality of fear pervades even the criminal law. The herd's spokesmen maintain that although criminals are a danger to society, they should not be punished, because that would be cruel; at most they should be locked up so that they can no longer do harm. Individuals who stand out from the herd are likewise condemned; mediocrity is now a virtue. Herd morality is egalitarian. In claiming that everyone is equal, the democratic spirit is the heir of Christianity. Sometimes it takes the form of socialism, which really wishes only to transform society by making the herd autonomous, without even nominal masters. And democracy in turn is threatened by anarchists, who openly aim at the destruction of society.

Acknowledging the many moralities, some coarser and others more refined, that have existed and now exist, Nietzsche distinguishes two basic types: master morality and slave morality (*BGE* 260). The noble (*vornehm*) person uses the categories 'good' and 'bad', where 'good' means 'noble' and 'bad' means 'contemptible'; these are not ethical judgements, but aesthetic descriptions. These categories are applied concretely to individuals, not abstractly to qualities. The noble person feels himself to be good because he has a sense of power, happiness, wealth. He despises people who are cowardly, timid, concerned with their own advantage; who are suspicious of others; who practise flattery and lying; who tamely put up with ill-treatment.

The noble person is not selfish, but if he helps others, it is not out of pity, but as a way of exerting his power. He does not feel compassion: Nietzsche quotes the hero of an Icelandic saga who says proudly: 'Odin put a hard heart in my breast' (*BGE* 260). Nietzsche's rejection of compassion may be thought one of the most repellent traits of his philosophy. Yet, as he himself points out, it has a long philosophical pedigree, from Plato to Kant (*GM* preface 5). The Stoics, with whose thought Nietzsche was familiar, held that the wise man should perform good actions without his emotions being troubled, 'with unruffled mind, and a countenance under control. The wise man, therefore, will not pity, but will succour, will benefit.'[35] Kant insists that a good action is not meritorious if it results from 'inclination' (for example the feeling of pity which makes one want to help someone), but only if it proceeds from an awareness of moral duty.[36] Nietzsche's argument – that compassion diminishes and weakens the person who feels it – is more Stoical than Kantian, but it is different from the mere callousness which admittedly he does occasionally express (*A* 2).

The noble do not acknowledge any universal values. They are conservative, respecting age and tradition. Their despicable counterparts are drawn to modern ideas about progress, which value the future more than the past. Dealing with one another, the noble follow a code of honour, and as their sense of honour is easily offended, this code also provides for revenge. The others, the slave types, are outside the honour code and may be treated as one pleases. The slaves themselves are utilitarians. They value the actions and qualities that they find useful: pity, helpfulness, patience, humility – but these qualities do not spring from kindness of heart; they are necessary for the slaves to survive under the rule of harsh masters. Yet somebody who is 'good' in the conventional modern sense – kindly and guileless – arouses some contempt even among the slaves, because such a person is not dangerous. Their masters *are* dangerous, and so the slaves fear and respect them, even while they hate them. Finally, the slave is incapable of reverence, because devotion to an ideal seems just another restriction on one's freedom, whereas the master feels reverence and awe for ideals.

It is for this reason that the ideal of courtly love, love as a spiritual passion, grew up among the feudal masters in medieval Provence.

Once one is familiar with the contrasting value-systems described here, it is easy to find examples. Dickens's *David Copperfield* turns on such an opposition. At school and later, David hero-worships the handsome, gifted, confident, charming, upper-class Steerforth, overlooking his egotism and his contempt for lower-class people. Steerforth's antithesis is Uriah Heep, an ambitious, crafty and physically odious lower-middle-class lawyer famous for his hypocritical professions of humility. Steerforth patronizes David as his inferior; Heep hates him as his superior, both in social rank and in virtue.

The Genealogy of Morals

The *Genealogy* is Nietzsche's first attempt since *The Birth of Tragedy* (unless one counts the essays in *Untimely Meditations*) to write a coherent monograph rather than a succession of linked aphorisms. It consists of three treatises, each divided into short aphoristic sections, and allowing many digressions, but it has a clear overall structure. It moves from primitive human societies in the first treatise to a bleak look into the future at the end of the third.

The title, however, has puzzled some commentators. What is a genealogy? Elaborate explanations have been given, which might lead one to think that 'genealogy' is a central Nietzschean concept.[37] In fact, however, the only occurrence of the word 'Genealogie' in Nietzsche's published writings is in the title of this book. And since Nietzsche describes other writers, with whom he disagrees, as putting forward 'genealogical hypotheses' (*GM* Prologue 4), it seems that he does not regard his method as categorically different from other attempts at writing the history of moral concepts.[38]

Nietzsche goes on to explain that other historians of morals, namely the British writers on whom his erstwhile friend Paul Rée drew for his *History of Moral Sentiments*, have based their history on hypotheses. Nietzsche, however, announces that instead of 'hypothesizing *into the blue*', his colour will be '*grey* – by that I mean what has been documented, what is really ascertainable, what has really existed, in short, the whole long hieroglyphic text, so difficult to decipher, of humanity's moral past!' (*GM* prologue 7). His history of morals will be based on documentary evidence. This includes ancient law codes, heroic epics and sagas, information about present-day 'primitive' societies, and the evidence of past values, which the etymologist can find preserved in words.[39] With these guides one can penetrate even beyond the beginnings of written history and find evidence for the ways of life and the moral values of our remote ancestors. The history Nietzsche thus offers is in large part a history of emotions, requiring us to enter imaginatively into the feelings of past cultures that were very different from our own.[40] It can thus be seen as continuing the efforts, made in Nietzsche's early publications, both to bring out how dissimilar the Greeks were to modern Europeans and to help us to transcend our narrow present by projecting ourselves into past mental worlds.

In the first treatise, Nietzsche leads us back to an ancient society of warriors living by the code he earlier called 'master morality'. As a classical scholar, he has clearly derived some clues from the Bronze Age society described in the *Iliad*; he also mentions Vikings, Germanic tribesmen and Japanese Samurai as examples, and elsewhere he says that the most important documents of 'master morality' are the Icelandic sagas (*cw* epilogue).[41] He takes for granted the common late nineteenth-century view that a society of fair-haired warriors, originating perhaps from South Russia, had in the second millennium BCE conquered dark-haired races inhabiting Europe and India, and had thus founded the civilization of ancient India and spread the Indo-European language group.[42] Hence the curious speculations about related words in Indo-European languages meaning 'fair-haired' and 'noble', and 'dark' and 'bad';

also that modern European democracy and socialism represent 'a huge *atavistic throwback*' which threatens 'the race of conquerors and *masters*, the Aryan race' (*GM* I 5).[43]

Conquerors like these, Nietzsche asserts, first created the state: 'some horde or other of blond predatory animals, a race of conquerors and masters [. . .] itself organized for war and with the strength to organize others, unhesitatingly lays its fearful paws on a population which may be hugely superior in numerical terms but remains shapeless and nomadic' (*GM* II 17). In attributing such violent origins to the state, Nietzsche, like Hume before him, breaks with the long tradition in political theory, from Hobbes to Rousseau, that traced political society back to a primordial social contract.[44]

Nietzsche's primeval warriors are honourable towards one another, but know no restrictions in dealing with their slaves. They never suffer from frustration, because they can always unleash their aggressive impulses on their inferiors. To the latter, they behave like beasts of prey, like the 'blond beast' (the lion) – 'as rejoicing monsters, capable of high spirits as they walk away without qualms from a horrific succession of murder, arson, violence, and torture, as if it were no more than a student prank, something for the poets to sing and celebrate for some time to come' (*GM* I 11).[45]

The primeval masters are beyond good and evil, or prior to such a distinction. They know only good and bad. They and their like are by definition good; whoever differs from them is bad. But the concept denoted by 'bad' is not a moral one. A bad slave is not seen as wicked, any more than a bad apple. The masters despise their slaves, but do not hate them. They are barbarians, capable of extreme cruelty, but at the same time they are overflowing with life-affirming energy and joy.

This noble caste, however, contains the seeds of its own downfall if it includes priests. The priest may originally have been a person whose physical weakness debarred him from sharing in the carefree aggression of his fellows. Inactive and brooding, he devised ritual practices such as fasting, sexual abstinence and self-isolation, which ran counter to the natural health of the warriors. Even worse, unable to release his frustration by external activity, he turned in upon himself and cultivated malice, hatred and cunning. Thus the priest was dangerous in a way that the warriors were not. But his character also acquired a depth of which the warriors were incapable. The warriors were thoughtless, even childish. In the person of the priest, humanity for the first time became '*an interesting animal*' (*GM* I 6).

The priest was therefore in a position to exert a new kind of authority over the slaves. The warrior kept them under by physical force; the priest controlled them by moral force. Under his tutelage, the concepts of good and evil, virtue and vice, developed. By some unexplained means, the slave revolt in morals took place. Towards their masters, the slaves felt *Ressentiment*: not just resentment, but a lingering, gnawing, insatiable desire for revenge. Yet in the slave revolt *Ressentiment* became creative.[46] The slaves revalued their masters' qualities and their own. The masters' self-satisfaction and pride became, in their eyes, sinful arrogance. The masters' violence and cruelty were condemned. The slaves' enforced obedience became a virtue. Their submissiveness was redefined as humility. Because they had no chance to take revenge on their masters, they described revenge as a sin.

Nietzsche maintains that this slave revolt originated among the Jews, whom he calls 'a priestly people' (alluding to the fact that after their return from Babylonian captivity in the sixth century BCE, the Jews were ruled by priests). Servile morals became the basis of Christianity. This is of course a one-sided and indeed malicious view of Christianity, but it is not unfounded, as one can see if one rereads the Beatitudes with Nietzsche's argument in mind: 'Blessed are the poor in spirit, for theirs is the kingdom of heaven'; 'Blessed are the meek; for they shall inherit the earth'

(Matthew 5:3, 5). One can see – anticipating Nietzsche's later polemics against Christianity – that these virtues are not advocated for their own sake, but as means of obtaining a prodigious reward, as Nietzsche himself remarks in a notebook (*KSA* XII 576). To show that priestly hatred survived in Christianity, Nietzsche quotes a long passage from the Church Father Tertullian (*c.* 160–*c.* 225 CE), who claims that the pleasures of the blessed souls in heaven will include contemplating the tortures of the damned (*GM* I 15).[47] And this religion of slaves, in which hatred is disguised by hypocrisy, conquered the Roman Empire. In the triumph of Christianity, the Jews took a successful revenge on their former oppressors. Nietzsche notes that in present-day Rome homage is paid to three Jewish men and one Jewish woman – to Jesus, Peter (allegedly the first Pope), Paul and the Virgin Mary.

Nietzsche ends by briefly indicating how the story continued. Plebeian resentment against masters found expression in the French Revolution, which inaugurated the age of democracy. But a sign pointing in a different, more hopeful direction, towards the restoration of the power of the few over the many, was the advent of Napoleon (*GM* I 16).

The second treatise, 'Guilt, Bad Conscience, and Related Matters', makes a fresh start by returning to prehistory and tracing different routes to the present. It undertakes to recount the development of responsibility: a story that begins with the animal living only in the moment, and ends with the modern, mature, sovereign individual, who discharges his responsibilities with guidance from his conscience. Nietzsche asks how nature managed to breed an animal that could make and keep promises. Such a being no longer inhabits the perpetual present of oblivious beasts, but remembers the past and plans for the future.

Nietzsche's explanation is extraordinarily convoluted. He offers two interwoven narratives combined with several sub-narratives. Both are based on the conviction that memory and responsibility developed only through prolonged and painful discipline. '"Something is branded in, so that it stays in the memory: only that which hurts incessantly is remembered" – this is a central proposition of the oldest (and unfortunately also the most enduring) psychology on earth' (*GM* II 3).

The first narrative concerns the development of guilt. It rests on the linguistic fact that in German *Schuld* means both 'guilt' and 'debt'. This homonymy encourages Nietzsche to put forward a thoroughly material genealogy of guilt. Guilt derives from debt. Originally, the injured party released his spontaneous anger against the person who had injured him. Then ancient societies set limits to the revenge an injured party could take, introducing a kind of tariff. The Old Testament prescribes 'eye for eye' (Exodus 21:24) – that is, if somebody knocks out one of your eyes, you are entitled in return to deprive him only of one eye, not of both. Or, instead of responding with equal violence, the offender could offer compensation in a quasi-commercial transaction (*GM* II 8). Later, the debt was owed not, or not only, to an individual, but to the entire community: the offence was understood to be against society, and its punishment was regulated by laws. In primitive tribal society the tribe was personified by its presumed ancestor, who was elevated into a god. Offences now had to be expiated by rituals and penances. Finally, after the invention of monotheism, the Christian God made his appearance, a 'maximal god', so powerful that no offence against him could ever be wiped out. Humanity would have been trapped in a nightmare of inescapable debt had not Christianity also invented the astounding notion that God sacrificed himself in order to pay humanity's debt. (As the Anglican hymn says, 'There was no other good enough/ To pay the price of sin.')

This narrative does not in itself explain how the material notion of debt was transmuted into the psychological notion of guilt, for which debt was increasingly felt to be only a metaphor.

So Nietzsche has to start again and explain how the joyful self-satisfaction of primitive warriors turned into the bad conscience, the feeling of guilt and sinfulness, that weighs down Christian believers. He suggests that when early humans first had to live in society and accept its restraints, the frustration of natural instincts led to their being driven inwards. 'Every instinct which does not vent itself externally *turns inwards* – this is what I call the *internalization* of man: it is at this point that what is later called the "soul" first develops in man' (*GM* II 16). Early humans were like the first sea creatures that began to live on land, painfully dragging themselves forward in an unfamiliar element, or like wild animals confined in zoos, vainly hurling themselves against the bars of their cages. Either then or later, the state came into being. It did not originate in a social contract but in an act of brutal conquest: a warrior elite imposed their rule on a more numerous but less organized population, and eventually, perhaps by the priestly methods evoked in the first treatise, made the latter feel inferior and hence sinful.

Both narratives, that of debt and that of guilt, involve cruelty. Some ancient law codes, such as the Roman Twelve Tables, allow the creditor to cut bits off the debtor's body (as Shylock wants to do in *The Merchant of Venice*). This might seem pointless, since the creditor could not thereby regain his lost property, but according to Nietzsche it satisfied the pleasure people always take in the spectacle, or better still in the infliction, of cruelty. The human animal must have been trained to remember by cruel punishments. Cruelty has been a source of pleasure throughout history. Savage punishments, such as breaking on the wheel, were prescribed in the German law code known as the *Carolina*, promulgated by Charles V in 1532; examples are myriad.[48] Various justifications have been offered for punishment – retribution, atonement, reformation, deterrence – but Nietzsche, having rapidly surveyed them, maintains that these merely disguise a basic pleasure in cruelty, which in turn is an expression of the will to power (*GM* II 13). The bad conscience is also a form of cruelty, which, having internalized a sense of sin, one exercises against oneself in order to punish oneself.

Nevertheless, Nietzsche finds something to be said for bad conscience, at least as a phase in moral history: 'Bad conscience is an illness, there is no doubt about it, but an illness in the same way that pregnancy is an illness' (*GM* II 19). It enormously developed humanity's inner life and created psychological depth. But it has also led humanity to deny its nature, to condemn the natural as such, and to seek salvation in an imaginary future world. How is humanity to be freed? Only by destruction: 'In order for a shrine to be set up, *another shrine must be broken into pieces*' (*GM* II 24). The destruction can only be carried out by a creative person capable of great love and great contempt, who will redeem humanity (Nietzsche uses the term *erlösen*, which has both economic and religious associations) from the curse that the otherworldly ideals have laid on it, somebody to whom Nietzsche is a mere disciple: Zarathustra the Godless.

The third treatise is not a historical narrative but an enquiry into an apparent contradiction found throughout history. That is asceticism, or self-denial. The ascetic rejects the pleasures of the senses and often even renounces sex and the opportunity to propagate the species. How can life thus turn against life, the will against the will, and, especially, what can be the function of sexual abstinence in a world propelled by the will to life and power? What can possibly be the evolutionary purpose served by celibacy?

Nietzsche distinguishes three types who practise asceticism: the artist, the philosopher and the priest. Each does so for a different reason. About artists, Nietzsche has rather little to say. They practise self-denial for many different reasons, and in any case they have no values of their own as artists, but take their values from a philosophical or religious authority. Thus Wagner absorbed

Schopenhauer's teaching that music was close to the Will, as the metaphysical principle governing the world, and accordingly developed a new kind of music-drama in which music was the primary element (*GM* III 5). He also learned from Schopenhauer an ascetic denigration of the senses that finds expression in his last work, *Parsifal* (1882), with its (for Nietzsche) nauseating Christian atmosphere and its exaltation of chastity. Nietzsche also deals a blow to ascetic ideals in aesthetics, namely to Kant's argument that the work of art demands from us disinterested contemplation free from desire. He contrasts Stendhal's pronouncement that beauty in art is 'une promesse de bonheur', a promise or foretaste of happiness.[49] Moreover, Nietzsche relates Kant's thesis to Schopenhauer's claim that the pleasure of art consists in temporarily liberating us from the pressure of the Will to which we are otherwise enslaved. In a typical below-the-belt argument, Nietzsche suggests that what Schopenhauer really meant was relief from the pressure of unsatisfied sexual desire. Thus while these sections contain only observations on particular artists and aestheticians, they suggest that, in denying the primacy of desire, such people are simply dishonest.

Philosophers, on the whole, come off better. Nietzsche observes that most of the great philosophers have been unmarried: Heraclitus, Plato, Descartes, Spinoza, Leibniz, Kant and Schopenhauer. (One could add Hobbes, Locke, Hume, Kierkegaard, Nietzsche himself and, from the twentieth century, Wittgenstein.) They remained single, not from any moral commitment to chastity, but for the entirely practical, down-to-earth reason that philosophy requires a full-time commitment to strenuous thinking and is incompatible with the cares of marriage and a household. Again, it is a result of their vocation that philosophers generally lead quiet, temperate lives and shun fame and the society of princes. For much of history, the philosophical disposition to question, to analyse and to suspend judgement met with social disapproval, so they were wise to keep their heads down. The ancient Indian Brahmans went further: they strengthened their authority by practising conspicuous feats of self-mortification that aroused fear and awe among the lay population. The asceticism of philosophers, therefore, is in general unproblematic.

The priest – who receives the bulk of attention in this treatise, before the last few sections turn to the asceticism of the scholar – is a much more complex figure. In him, life turns decisively against life, sex, self-perpetuation, pleasure, indeed, against the world; as in the Hindu texts known as the Vedantas, he may reject the whole material world as an error or an illusion (*GM* III 12). And yet the priest's hostility to life must in some strange way serve the interests of life.

Nietzsche's explanation lies in the fact that most human beings are sick. Unlike other animals, which are well adjusted to their environment, man is always uncomfortable, discontented, anxious for something better; man is by definition '*the* sick animal' (*GM* III 13). The great mass of humanity are unhappy, unwell, incapable of taking pleasure in life, even consumed by disgust and loathing. Just occasionally, however, thanks to a lucky chance, a strong, healthy, happy human being is born (Nietzsche's favourite example is Goethe). These exceptions are in danger from the sick. The sick may conspire together to destroy the healthy, not by a mere physical attack, but by denouncing the healthy as impious, evil and sinful, and thus poisoning the wellsprings of health. This is the slave revolt in morals, evoked in the first treatise, by which the slaves reinterpreted the values of the masters in order to condemn them.

But there is another danger, and it comes from the healthy. Just because they are strong and generous, the healthy are liable to feel compassion for the sick and want to tend and cure them. That would be a fatal mistake. Not only are the sick incurable, but they may infect the healthy with their own loathing of life and drive their would-be saviours to despair. And without the healthy, there will be nobody to arrest the degeneration of the human species, which Nietzsche sees proceeding rapidly, and to bring about a new, stronger humanity – one that, we may say, can respond to the message of Zarathustra.

This is where the priest comes in. He, the enemy of life, unwittingly serves life. He corrals the sick together as a flock, of which he is the shepherd (Nietzsche is here maliciously adopting the imagery of the Gospels). He can do so because he is sick too, and thus understands his followers, but his will to power is stronger than theirs. He professes to be a physician, but he soothes his followers' wounds only to drip poison into them. He keeps his flock in a state of low vitality, which Nietzsche compares to the hibernation practised by many animals. He prescribes mechanical activity (prayer) and allows them small pleasures such as mutual services under the name of brotherly love. He encourages them to feel guilty and sinful, and to regard the flock as more important than any of the individuals composing it.

The flock are not only unhappy, but probably suffer from a variety of physical ailments resulting from a bad diet or poor circulation. Whether their pain is physical or emotional, they seek to dull it and distract themselves by cultivating other emotions. Ironically, these emotions may themselves be painful. The priest encourages his followers to torment themselves by examining their past lives and thinking how sinful they are. That at least gives their unhappiness meaning, for there is nothing worse than *meaningless* suffering. They seek someone to blame for their unhappiness. The obvious course would be to attack the healthy as scapegoats, but here the priest shows his value for the process of life. He tells his flock that they themselves are to blame for their unhappiness, because of their sinful natures. If a sickly sheep complains: 'I am suffering: someone must be to blame,' the priest replies: 'Just so, my sheep! Someone must be to blame: but you yourself are this someone, you alone are to blame – *you alone are to blame for yourself!'* (*GM* III 15). To distract them further, he allows them various kinds of emotional debauch: repentance for their imagined sins, contrition, terror, self-punishment, self-mortification with the scourge and the hair shirt. Far from resenting the pain he inflicts on them, they demand more pain. And while they do so, they leave the healthy in peace.

This account of religious practices – not only Christian, but Hindu and Buddhist – refers constantly to physiology. If at the beginning of *Beyond Good and Evil* Nietzsche wanted psychology to supersede philosophy as the queen of the sciences, he now, towards the end of *The Genealogy of Morals*, subsumes psychology into physiology. The unhappiness of the religious masses is explained as physiological, and their search for scapegoats as a physiological effect. Thus Nietzsche picks up again the concept of *Ressentiment* that he used in the first treatise, but now gives it a medical basis (*GM* III 17). He goes further and sketches a medical history of Europe. Europe has suffered periodical waves of physiological depression. The cause may be the mingling of different races or classes; it may be a bad diet (Nietzsche condemns both alcoholism and vegetarianism);[50] it may be blood-poisoning through malaria and syphilis. By encouraging people to believe in their own sinfulness and engage in penitential practices, the ascetic priest has made things worse, causing such dramatic outbreaks of mass hysteria as the well-attested dancing manias of the late Middle Ages and the witch craze that afflicted early modern Europe. It seems, therefore, that the ascetic priest exercises his tyranny less through psychological insight than by manipulating his followers' physiology.

The *Genealogy* ends by examining the possibility of knowledge and the motives that animate people dedicated to knowledge: scholars and scientists. An apparent digression earlier, raising the theme of perspective, turns out to be a prelude to the closing sections. Here Nietzsche's key point is that there is no knowledge entirely free from emotion, or 'affect'.[51] One can attain objectivity not by trying to exclude all affect, but by apprehending a variety of affects (*GM* III 12).

This form of knowledge is particularly appropriate to *The Genealogy of Morals*. For Nietzsche is there trying to reconstruct, with the aid both of documents and of imagination, past moral codes and their attendant ways of living.[52] To understand them, you must imagine what it felt like to be a joyfully murderous aristocrat or a cowering resentful slave, or to enjoy seeing a criminal tortured to death. *The Genealogy of Morals* thus exemplifies a way of doing history that differs widely from the detachment practised by professional historians that Nietzsche criticizes in 'On the Use and Disadvantage of History'. It fulfils Nietzsche's earlier demand for 'a *history* of ethical and religious sentiments' (*WS* 16). And to carry conviction, it needs to be comprehensive: there would be little value in recounting the origins of Christianity solely from a Christian perspective. One has rather to move among different perspectives, 'to have all the arguments for and against *at one's disposal* and to suspend or implement them at will' (*GM* III 12).

Nietzsche is therefore not an epistemological sceptic. He affirms that reasonably accurate knowledge is possible, although difficult to attain. Hence he is able to examine what motivates people to seek knowledge. The knowledge attained by science and scholarship (*Wissenschaft*) is often unwelcome. Copernicus' discovery that the earth is not the centre of the universe has diminished humanity's sense of its own importance. Modern historians deny that history has any meaning or purpose. All branches of learning profess to be value-free; they only describe phenomena and agree that we are merely, as Nietzsche puts it elsewhere, 'clever animals on a dying star'.[53] The will to truth, the desire to find truth at any cost, is really the ultimate form of the ascetic ideal.

Such a will animates modern science. Scientists accept that reality is bleak, cruel, comfortless, that we are merely short-lived animals on a fragile planet, but regard it as an imperative to extend and deepen such knowledge. In a related passage from *Beyond Good and Evil*, Nietzsche sketches the history of religious cruelty: first, people sacrificed their most valuable possessions to their gods; then they sacrificed their natural instincts to the Christian God; finally, in the age of scientific atheism, they sacrifice 'everything comforting, holy, healing, all hope, all faith in a concealed harmony, in a future bliss and justice' (*BGE* 55) and get *nothing* in return. Hence the scholarly enquirer is the purest example of asceticism:

> One sees a sad, hard, but determined gaze – an eye which *looks out*, as an isolated Arctic explorer looks out (perhaps in order not to look in? in order not to look back? . . .). Here is snow, here life is silenced, the last crows whose cries can still be heard are called 'Why?', 'In vain!', 'Nada!' (*GM* III 26)

The crows' message is that nothing has any value or any point.

The frozen waste of asceticism is also, at the same time and to an even higher degree, *'nihilistic'* (*GM* III 26). The word 'nihilism' appears only a few times in Nietzsche's published works, much more often in his notebooks, and is particularly associated with Russia (*GS* 347, *GM* III 26). A long series of entries from the winter of 1887–8, headed 'On the Psychology of the Nihilist', quotes extensively from Dostoevsky's *The Devils* and mentions the characters Stavrogin and Kirilov (*KSA* XIII 142–50). By nihilism, Nietzsche does not just mean the passive indifference to ideals shown by the 'last men' in *Zarathustra*. Nihilism is a direction of the will, a 'will to nothing' (*GM* III 26). If you really think nothing matters, you may as well turn to wanton destruction and blow everything up, as Dostoevsky's nihilist revolutionaries plan to do. For, as Nietzsche concludes, the will is perversely unstoppable: 'man would rather will nothingness than will nothing!' (*GM* III 28).

Anti-Christianity

The three books Nietzsche wrote in the last year before his collapse – *Twilight of the Idols, The Antichrist* and the eccentric self-portrait *Ecce Homo* – insistently repeat his basic doctrine, albeit with some elaborations. The fundamental principle is 'life', which is either ascending (growing stronger) or descending (becoming weak and degenerate). Life resides in the body, much more than in the mind: hence the enormous importance Nietzsche assigns to physiology, and to the care and cultivation of the body through diet, exercise and hygiene. Strong, healthy people follow their instincts. They enjoy 'a fuller, more prodigal, more overflowing life' than others (*TI* 'Expeditions' 37). Such a person is an egotist. He is happy to stand out as an individual, distinct from others, and to evoke the 'pathos of distance' (ibid.). He enjoys war and danger (*TI* 'Morality' 3, 'Expeditions' 38). He does not feel compassion, for compassion depresses one's spirits, and its effect is to keep alive degenerate people who ought to perish.

Life starts to decline when people no longer trust their instincts. To deny one's instincts is the beginning of decadence (*TI* 'Socrates' 12). One strives against one's own physiology, one's own health. Feeling ill, one seeks someone or something to blame and finds it in evil spirits; or in one's own natural impulses, which are now revalued as evil; or, as with modern socialists, in the supposed injustice of society. One readily puts oneself in the hands of the priest, who exercises his power as described in the third treatise of *The Genealogy of Morals*. The decadent denies life, regards compassion as a virtue and makes equality a social ideal. Decadence generates other errors, such as modern marriage based on love instead of power (*TI* 'Expeditions' 39) and female emancipation, which appeals only to women unable or unfit to bear children (*EH* 5). The few strong people who are born by lucky chances are demonized. The 'criminal type' is actually a strong person made sick by modern society; Nietzsche finds support for this claim in the account Dostoevsky gives in *The House of the Dead* of his fellow convicts in Siberia.[54]

The decadence that threatens to ruin the modern world is principally the fault of Christianity. In *The Antichrist* Nietzsche amplifies, and simplifies, the critique of Christianity that runs through his earlier writings. Now drawing extensively on Wellhausen's studies of the Old Testament, he maintains that the rot set in even in Old Testament times. Originally, God was a projection of ancient humanity's feeling of power; he was imagined as both good and evil, the source of both benefits and damage. A later dualistic outlook undertook 'the unnatural castration of a god into a god merely of the good', a God of the weak (*A* 16). After the Jews' return from Babylonian exile, they were ruled by priests, parasites on society, who consolidated their power by presenting their own will as the will of God.[55] Christianity enormously extended the falsification of nature which Judaism had begun. Nature, instinct and above all sexuality were classified as evil. A whole host of baseless notions about guilt, punishment and redemption were invented to keep believers submissive.

Discussing the enigmatic individual Jesus, Nietzsche performs an adroit move which takes Jesus out of this narrative. On Nietzsche's reading of the Gospels, Jesus had no doctrine, no message. He illustrated a way of living. He felt an immediate, blissful sense of unity with life, which he could only express by metaphors such as 'light', 'truth', 'life' or 'the kingdom of God': 'What are the "glad tidings"? True life, eternal life is found – it is not promised, it is here, it is *within you*: as life lived in love, in love without deduction or exclusion' (*A* 29).[56] From a physiological viewpoint, Nietzsche adds, such a person is best described by the word 'idiot'. By this he means not a stupid person, but the kind of holy fool evoked by Dostoevsky in *The Idiot*; there is no direct evidence that Nietzsche had read this novel, but it seems to pervade *The Antichrist*.

Such a Jesus cannot have planned to found a religion. By his very existence, this 'holy anarchist' represented a danger to the priesthood, who took care to have him crucified. In response, his disciples sought revenge. They falsified Jesus' words into a doctrine and filled the Gospels with threats of punishment (as Nietzsche shows with the help of revealing quotations, *A* 45). St Paul in particular was 'a genius of hatred' (*A* 42), 'the greatest of all apostles of revenge' (*A* 45). Thanks to him, Jesus' death was reinterpreted as a sacrifice, 'and that in its most repulsive, barbaric form, the sacrifice of the *innocent man* for the sins of the guilty!' (*A* 41). The new religion was supported by the bogus promise of personal immortality. Reason was condemned (Nietzsche quotes 'Hath not God made foolish the wisdom of the world?' 1 Corinthians 1:20, *A* 45). The 'highest states' for Christians were forms of epilepsy (*A* 21, 51; Nietzsche means Paul's hallucination on the road to Damascus, and mystical experiences more generally).[57] Christianity acquired all sorts of accretions, such as the fable of the Virgin Birth. The story that the Virgin Mary was impregnated by the Holy Spirit is a version of the Greek myth of Amphitryon (whose wife Alcmene was seduced by the god Zeus and gave birth to Hercules; *A* 34). Above all, Christianity became a system of guilt, punishment, self-mortification and imaginary redemption, operated by priests for the purpose of making humanity incurably sick. Modern Europe has not recovered: Christian ideals have been transmuted into those of humanitarianism and equality, and the fiction of the 'moral world order' (*A* 26).

Along the way, Christianity destroyed the culture of the ancient world, an intolerable loss: 'The whole labour of the ancient world *in vain*: I have no words to express my feelings at something so dreadful' (*A* 59). Later it destroyed the rich cultural world of Moorish Spain. And just when the noble values were about to triumph in the Renaissance, and there was even a possibility that Christianity might be abolished, along came the brutal philistine

Martin Luther to strengthen it by means of the Reformation. Nietzsche concludes: 'The Christian Church has left nothing untouched by its depravity, it has made of every value a disvalue [*einen Unwerth*], of every truth a lie, of every kind of integrity a vileness of soul' (*A* 62).

To replace these destructive values, Nietzsche repeatedly proposes a 'revaluation of all values' (*Umwerthung aller Werthe*).[58] As an example of future revaluation, Nietzsche first refers to the Christian claim that virtue is the reward of happiness, and then maintains that in future, virtue will be the *result* of happiness (*TI* 'Errors' 2): happy people will spontaneously conform to their community's standards of virtue. It may be that the concept of conscience will survive, but in reverse, so that following one's instincts will be praiseworthy but any hankering after otherworldly values will generate guilt (*GM* II 24). Usually, however, Nietzsche assumes that the conscience will vanish along with all the other apparatus of Christianity. Future people, overflowing with well-being and not depressed by compassion for sufferers, will spontaneously treat their fellows in a suitably noble or *vornehm* manner.

This happiness will be reserved for the strong. First, Europe must be saved from terminal decline by being brought under the rule of an elite. Nietzsche has already discerned a sign of hope in Napoleon, the last European with an absolute power of commanding (*BGE* 199). With more such people, society can be reshaped. In order to give primacy to culture, it must have the shape of a pyramid, with a small elite at the top (*A* 57). The caste society of India, codified in the ancient Laws of Manu, has its flaws (inbreeding), but is far preferable to the egalitarianism that Europe has inherited from Christianity.[59]

The strong must be restored to dominance. However, the subordinate castes need not be kept down by oppression. Modern egalitarianism would be replaced by an acceptance of the noble caste as natural superiors and hence as legitimate rulers. The great majority of people 'exist for service and general utility and [. . .] *may* exist only for that purpose' (*BGE* 61). While the noble caste enjoyed the leisure necessary to cultivate the arts, their inferiors might work contentedly, feeling that their own existence was justified by serving culture. They would be 'multifarious, garrulous, weak-willed and highly employable workers who *need* a master, a commander, as they need their daily bread' (*BGE* 242). They would look up to their masters with the 'pathos of distance', the feelings of reverence generated by accepting their relatively low station in life (*BGE* 257, *A* 43). This would be slavery, but 'in the *subtlest* sense' (*BGE* 242), because they would so thoroughly have internalized their social inferiority.

What has been called 'the gentle side' of Nietzsche's thinking is accompanied by a brutal side.[60] The noble rulers, in whom we may see the Overhumans of the future, will be tyrants. They will fight tremendous, more than Napoleonic wars, 'such as have never yet been on earth' (*EH* 'Destiny' 1). They will enact a 'struggle for mastery over the whole earth' which Nietzsche calls 'great politics' (*BGE* 208).

The future of society and humanity must no longer be entrusted to evolutionary processes, which are as likely to lead to degeneration as to improvement, but should be the result of deliberate action. After denouncing the degenerate state of Christian and democratic Europe, Nietzsche says that the future of humanity should not be left to chance, but should be shaped by the will:

To teach man the future of man as his *will*, as dependent on a human will, and to prepare for great enterprises and collective experiments in discipline and breeding so as to make an end of that gruesome dominion of chance and nonsense that has hitherto been called 'history' – the nonsense of the 'greatest number' is only its latest form – : for that a new kind of philosopher and commander will some time be needed, in face of whom whatever has existed on earth of hidden, dreadful and benevolent spirits may well look pale and dwarfed. (*BGE* 203)

For the moment, the phrase that most demands attention here is 'discipline and breeding' (*Zucht und Züchtung*). The wordplay in the original text blurs the distinction between two kinds of breeding: that imparted by strict education, whose beneficiaries may be called 'well-bred', and that undertaken by animal breeders who try to produce improved strains of dogs and rabbits. Similarly, Zarathustra urges his hearers to form 'a new nobility' and become 'progenitors and cultivators and sowers of the future' (*z* III 12/12), where the discreet translation 'cultivators' disguises *Züchter* (breeders). There has been much dispute about whether Nietzsche was advocating eugenics, that is, deliberate selective breeding. He certainly read about it.[61] Moreover, in Nietzsche's day and long after, eugenics, put forward by Darwin's cousin Francis Galton in 1883, enjoyed considerable scientific and political respectability on both the right and the left.[62] Many contemporaries understood Nietzsche as a eugenicist, and as combining eugenics with Darwinism.[63] The breeding denoted by *Züchtung*, however, need not imply biological programmes such as the Nazis later attempted. The version of evolutionary theory that Nietzsche favoured was not Darwin's but Lamarck's, in which acquired characteristics can be inherited. *Züchtung* might therefore be accomplished by a thorough-going programme of education, like the ancient Greek *paideia*.[64]

Nietzsche goes further, however, and suggests that the cultivation of an aristocracy should include control over the choice of marriage partners and hence a form of positive eugenics. He is talking about the control exerted in aristocratic communities such as the Venetian Republic or the ancient Greek *polis*:

It does so with severity, indeed it wants severity; every aristocratic morality is intolerant, in the education of the young, in the measures it takes with respect to women, in marriage customs, in the relations between young and old, in the penal laws (which are directed only at variants) – it counts intolerance itself among the virtues under the name 'justice'. (*BGE* 262)[65]

Besides breeding better people, future rulers will get rid of worse people. The mediocre are useful, but the degenerate harm humanity as a whole. The unfortunate – 'the sick, the degenerate, the fragile, [. . .] those who are bound to suffer' (*BGE* 62) – are carefully preserved and treated with compassion by Christianity, which thereby promotes 'the *corruption of the European race*' (*BGE* 62). Since the unfortunate cannot be cured, they should be pushed further downhill: 'The weak and ill-constituted shall perish: first principle of *our* philanthropy. And one shall help them to do so' (*A* 2). When an organism goes wrong, the physiologist cuts out the degenerate part (*EH* 'Dawn' 2). Those at work to raise mankind, the 'party of life', will undertake 'the merciless annihilation of everything that is degenerate and parasitical' (*EH* 'BT' 4).

Do these passages justify calling Nietzsche the 'godfather of fascism'? In some obvious ways, yes. Ideas about degeneracy were common coin in late nineteenth-century Europe, but recommendations for destroying the 'degenerate' were part of fascism. The systematic annihilation of unwanted parts of the population (Jews, Roma and Sinti, homosexuals) seems here to be legitimized in advance. More generally, much in Nietzsche's published writings lent itself to appropriation by the far right: as we have seen, he denounces democracy, socialism, feminism and equal rights; he warns against 'degeneration' (*Entartung*, for example *BGE* 203); he praises hierarchy and violence and seeks to justify slavery. One can understand why so many of his expositors have wanted to ignore or downplay these assertions. Yet they are integral to Nietzsche's philosophy.

Historians have demonstrated that ideas and phrases from Nietzsche formed part of the official culture of the Third Reich and permeated its educational and legal systems.[66] Nietzsche's attacks on democracy, humanitarianism and Christianity, and his advocacy of manly, warlike values, were welcomed and constantly repeated. Some notorious passages, mostly but not all from *The Will to Power*, were cited to justify euthanasia and a positive programme of eugenics.

On the other hand, existing fascism failed, in important ways, to match Nietzsche's visions. Fascist rulers were not the Renaissance-style tyrants and supremely gifted people that Nietzsche imagined. They came from those parts of the population that he dismissed as at best mediocre, at worst 'rabble'. They were not aristocrats, exercising legitimate rule over a submissive and industrious herd, but political leaders who controlled mass parties by shameless manipulation and deceit. Rather than Overhumans, they resembled Nietzsche's sick priests, who can control their flock because they share their followers' sickness.

To be fair to Nietzsche, one should ask about his motives in writing these shocking passages (and worse ones in *The Will to Power* which he did not intend to publish). Did he really enjoy the thought of mass murder? It is more likely that he failed to consider how his fantasies would work out in practice. Solitary and living largely inside his own head, he just did not connect with other people's experience. If so, his fantasies of power, although still reprehensible, are not so much wicked as frivolous. Although Nietzsche, in these passages, *thinks* he has a momentous mission to save civilization, he is fundamentally not being serious.

There are other reasons why Nietzsche appealed to so many readers. Let us turn away for a moment from his fantasies of power. Many contemporaries agreed with Nietzsche that nineteenth-century science had disclosed a bleak, comfortless universe devoid of purpose and meaning. Bertrand Russell wrote in 1903:

That Man is the product of causes which had no prevision
of the end they were achieving; that his origin, his growth,
his hopes and fears, his loves and his beliefs, are but the
outcome of accidental collocations of atoms; that no fire, no
heroism, no intensity of thought and feeling, can preserve
an individual life beyond the grave; that all the labours of
the ages, all the devotion, all the inspiration, all the noonday
brightness of human genius, are destined to extinction
in the vast death of the solar system, and that the whole
temple of Man's achievement must inevitably be buried
beneath the debris of a universe in ruins – all these things,
if not quite beyond dispute, are yet so nearly certain, that
no philosophy which rejects them can hope to stand.[67]

Subtract the bombast and the 'atoms' (Nietzsche rejected
materialism and positivism), and you have here the grim, empty
universe of modern science, which, in Nietzsche's view, offered a
fatal temptation to nihilism.

Yet the universe that Nietzsche offers us is also empty. It is an
infinite Heraclitean flux in which our imagination constructs small,
transient islands of apparent solidity. There is no transcendent
meaning, no providence, no moral absolutes, no absolutes of any
kind; in heady moments, there may not even be truth. But these
negatives do not mean loss: they mean liberation. Freed from the
illusions that religion and its derivatives have imposed on us, we
can – in Wallace Stevens's words – step 'barefoot into reality'.[68] And
reality, the eternal energy of life, is not dismal, but exhilarating. It
offers trials and tests in which the strong will rejoice while nobody
cares about the weak. The greatest trial is of course accepting that
once our cosmos has come to an end, it will start all over again and
recur eternally.

This is compelling as a poetic vision. It has much in common
with the intuitions of Blake – 'Energy is Eternal Delight' – and

Goethe, who in *Faust Part One* presents the world as an eternal interplay of creation and destruction.[69] How valid it is as a philosophy, or a creed to live by, is something each reader must decide independently. Few people now believe that the world follows a script written by God. But there is no need to substitute another playbook written by Nietzschean philosophers. It is possible to accept, without making a drama out of it, that the meaning of life lies in the here and now: in our interaction with other people, and in such projects as sustaining a marriage, raising a family, writing a book, making a career. In proclaiming a cosmic doctrine, Nietzsche and his spokesman Zarathustra have not eluded the dead God of Christianity, but have replaced him with his antithesis. The escape route from both is offered by the Enlightenment – not only the scientific search for truth, and the Voltairean campaign against clerical tyranny, but the strand of the Enlightenment that focused on sympathy, on shared emotion, on the ability to put oneself in someone else's shoes, and – fortunately – on the compassion that philosophers from Plato to Nietzsche have decried.[70]

References

Introduction

1   Letter to Lady Gregory, 26 December 1902, in *The Collected Letters of W. B. Yeats*, vol. III, ed. John Kelly and Ronald Schuchard (Oxford, 1994), p. 284.

2   For Nietzsche's reception in the English-speaking world, see Patrick Bridgwater, *Nietzsche in Anglosaxony* (Leicester, 1972); in France, Douglas Smith, *Transvaluations: Nietzsche in France, 1872–1972* (Oxford, 1996); in Germany, Steven E. Aschheim, *The Nietzsche Legacy in Germany, 1890–1990* (Berkeley, CA, 1992); besides numerous specialized studies, some of which are listed in the Bibliography.

3   Alexander Nehamas, *Nietzsche: Life as Literature* (Cambridge, MA, 1985), pp. 23–4.

4   Paul Bishop, ed., *A Companion to Friedrich Nietzsche: Life and Works* (Rochester, NY, 2012), p. 199.

5   Mazzino Montinari, 'Nietzsches Nachlaß von 1885 bis 1888 oder Textkritik und Wille zur Macht', in *Nietzsche lesen* (Berlin, 1982), pp. 92–119; cf. Bishop, *Companion*, p. 318.

6   Richard Schacht, *Nietzsche* (London, 1983); Nehamas, *Nietzsche: Life as Literature*.

7   An exception is Christopher Janaway, *Beyond Selflessness: Reading Nietzsche's 'Genealogy'* (Oxford, 2007), pp. 95–8.

8   Bernard Reginster, *The Affirmation of Life: Nietzsche on Overcoming Nihilism* (Cambridge, MA, 2006), p. 67.

9   Walter Kaufmann, *Nietzsche: Philosopher, Psychologist, Antichrist*, 4th edn (Princeton, NJ, 1974). For the presence of Nazism in Heidegger's readings, see Aschheim, *The Nietzsche Legacy*, pp. 262–70.

10 See David R. Allison, ed., *The New Nietzsche: Contemporary Styles of Interpretation* (Cambridge, MA, 1985).

11 For example Schacht, *Nietzsche*; Maudemarie Clark, *Nietzsche on Truth and Philosophy* (Cambridge, 1990).

12 See especially Christian J. Emden, *Friedrich Nietzsche and the Politics of History* (Cambridge, 2008); Robert C. Holub, *Nietzsche in the Nineteenth Century: Social Questions and Philosophical Interventions* (Philadelphia, PA, 2018).

13 See Thomas Brobjer, *Nietzsche's Philosophical Context: An Intellectual Biography* (Urbana, IL, 2008). Some of Nietzsche's books and annotations can be seen in the Archive's online exhibition 'Nietzsche liest. Bücher und Lektüren Nietzsches', at https://ausstellungen. deutsche-digitale-bibliothek.de/nietzsche-liest, accessed 15 February 2021.

14 See Gregory Moore, *Nietzsche, Biology and Metaphor* (Cambridge, 2002); Robin Small, *Nietzsche in Context* (Aldershot, 2001); Christian J. Emden, *Nietzsche's Naturalism: Philosophy and the Life Sciences in the Nineteenth Century* (Cambridge, 2014).

15 *Kant: Political Writings*, ed. Hans Reiss, trans. H. B. Nisbet, 2nd edn (Cambridge, 1991), p. 54.

1 The Philologist

1 For 'total institutions', see Erving Goffman, *Asylums* (New York, 1961).

2 Ronald Hayman, *Nietzsche: A Critical Life* (London, 1980), p. 28.

3 Cf. for example C. S. Lewis, *Surprised by Joy* (London, 1955).

4 Contrast George J. Stack, *Nietzsche and Emerson: An Elective Affinity* (Athens, OH, 1992), p. 5, with Thomas Brobjer, *Nietzsche's Philosophical Context: An Intellectual Biography* (Urbana, IL, 2008), p. 22.

5 *The Portable Emerson*, ed. Jeffrey S. Cramer (London, 2014), p. 157.

6 Benedetta Zavatta, 'Nietzsche, Emerson und das Selbstvertrauen', *Nietzsche-Studien*, 35 (2006), pp. 274–97.

7 Quoted in Curt Paul Janz, *Friedrich Nietzsche: Biographie*, 3 vols (Munich, 1978), vol. I, p. 108.

8 Quoted ibid., pp. 137–8.

9   Charlie Huenemann, 'Nietzsche's Illness', in *The Oxford Handbook of Nietzsche*, ed. John Richardson and Ken Gemes (Oxford, 2013), pp. 63–80.

10 Jacob Burckhardt, *The Greeks and Greek Civilization*, trans. Sheila Stern (London, 1998); Oswyn Murray, 'Burckhardt and the Archaic Age', in *Jacob Burckhardt und die Griechen*, ed. Leonhard Burckhardt and Hans-Joachim Gehrke (Basel and Munich, 2006), pp. 247–61.

11 Janz, *Friedrich Nietzsche: Biographie*, vol. I, p. 209.

12 Cf. his description of autumn in Turin in 1888 as 'a Claude Lorrain imagined as infinite, every day of similar boundless perfection' (*EH* '*GD*' 3); similarly in the letter to Meta von Salis, 14 November 1888: 'a Claude Lorrain in permanence'. For *Der Nachsommer*, see *WS* 109.

13 Arthur Schopenhauer, *The World as Will and Representation*, Book III, ch. 36. Nietzsche borrows Schopenhauer's term 'Fabrikwaare' in 'Schopenhauer as Educator': see *UM*, p. 127 ('factory products'), though he claims there, not that most people are mediocre by nature, but that they aspire to nothing higher.

14 See the essay 'On Schopenhauer' [1868], in *Willing and Nothingness: Schopenhauer as Nietzsche's Educator*, ed. Christopher Janaway (Oxford, 1998), pp. 258–65.

15 F. A. Lange, *History of Materialism*, trans. Ernest Chester Thomas, 3 vols, 3rd edn (London, 1925), vol. II, p. 158.

16 Ibid., p. 216.

17 Ibid., pp. 231–2.

18 Janz, *Friedrich Nietzsche: Biographie*, vol. I, p. 254.

19 Lionel Gossman, *Basel in the Age of Burckhardt: A Study in Unseasonable Ideas* (Chicago, IL, 2000).

20 In 1888 he described her as 'by far the most aristocratic nature' (*EH* 'Wise' 3). On the brink of madness, he associated her with Ariadne, the mythical bride of Dionysus (to Burckhardt, 6 January 1889); cf. Carol Diethe, *Nietzsche's Women: Beyond the Whip* (Berlin, 1996), pp. 35–6.

21 See Dieter Borchmeyer, 'Wagner and Nietzsche', in *Wagner Handbook*, ed. Ulrich Müller and Peter Wapnewski (Cambridge, MA, 1992), pp. 327–42.

2 The Cultural Critic

1 D. A. Russell and M. Winterbottom, eds, *Ancient Literary Criticism* (Oxford, 1972), p. 95.

2 See Hugh Lloyd-Jones, 'Nietzsche and the Study of the Ancient World', in *Studies in Nietzsche and the Classical Tradition*, ed. James C. O'Flaherty, Timothy F. Sellner and Robert M. Helm (Chapel Hill, NC, 1976), pp. 1–15; M. S. Silk and J. P. Stern, *Nietzsche on Tragedy* (Cambridge, 1981).

3 Erwin Rohde, *Psyche: The Cult of Souls and the Belief in Immortality among the Greeks*, trans. W. B. Hillis (London, 1925).

4 E. R. Dodds, *The Greeks and the Irrational* (Berkeley, CA, 1951), p. 105. Dodds admits to 'standing . . . on the shoulders of Rohde', p. 65.

5 See Martin A. Ruehl, '*Politeia* 1871: Young Nietzsche on the Greek State', in *Nietzsche and Antiquity*, ed. Paul Bishop (Rochester, NY, 2004), pp. 79–97; 'Ruthless Renaissance: Burckhardt, Nietzsche, and the Violent Birth of the Modern Self ', in *The Italian Renaissance in the German Historical Imagination* (Cambridge, 2015), pp. 58–104.

6 Werner Kaegi, *Jacob Burckhardt: Eine Biographie*, 7 vols (Basel, 1947–82), vol. VII, pp. 9, 44–5; Lionel Gossman, *Basel in the Age of Burckhardt: A Study in Unseasonable Ideas* (Chicago, IL, 2000), p. 303.

7 Modern scholarship has confirmed Burckhardt's picture: Arnaldo Momigliano, 'Introduction to the Griechische Kulturgeschichte by Jacob Burckhardt', in *Essays in Ancient and Modern Historiography* (Oxford, 1977), pp. 295–305; Oswyn Murray, 'Burckhardt and the Archaic Age', in *Jacob Burckhardt und die Griechen*, ed. Leonhard Burckhardt and Hans-Joachim Gehrke (Basel, 2006), pp. 247–61.

8 Letter to Gottfried Kinkel, 19 April 1845, in Jacob Burckhardt, *Briefe*, 11 vols (Basel, 1949–94), vol. II, p. 158.

9 Sophocles, *The Theban Plays*, trans. E. F. Watling (Harmondsworth, 1947), p. 109.

10 Theognis in *Greek Elegiac Poetry*, trans. Douglas E. Gerber (Cambridge, MA, 2014), p. 425.

11 Cf. the contrast between medieval feudalism and nineteenth-century industrialism drawn by Thomas Carlyle in *Past and Present* (1843).

12 'State', 784: Nietzsche mentions the atrocities practised during
    the revolution in Corcyra, described by Thucydides, *The Peloponnesian
    War*, trans. Rex Warner (Harmondsworth, 1954), p. 257.

13 Hesiod, *Works and Days*, ll. 11–26, in *Theogony, Works and
    Days, Testimonia*, trans. G. W. Most (Cambridge, MA, 2006),
    pp. 87, 89.

14 Robert C. Holub, *Nietzsche in the Nineteenth Century: Social Questions
    and Philosophical Interventions* (Philadelphia, PA, 2018), p. 21; cf.
    W. H. Bruford, *The German Tradition of Self-Cultivation: 'Bildung'
    from Humboldt to Thomas Mann* (Cambridge, 1975).

15 Franz Overbeck, *Über die Christlichkeit der heutigen Theologie* (repr.
    Darmstadt, 1963), p. 119. Overbeck pays tribute to Nietzsche's
    friendship in his introduction to a later edition, ibid., pp. 13–19. On
    Overbeck, his friendship with Nietzsche and his polemical book, see
    Gossman, *Basel*, pp. 416–23.

16 As in the Ringstrasse in Vienna. See Carl E. Schorske, *Fin-de-Siècle
    Vienna: Politics and Culture* (New York, 1980), pp. 24–114.

3 The Aphorist

1 Christopher Janaway, ed., *Willing and Nothingness: Schopenhauer as
   Nietzsche's Educator* (Oxford, 1998), p. 25.

2 Spir (1837–1890) is the 'excellent logician' quoted in *HA* I 18 as
   formulating the basic law of perception that the subject understands
   each object as self-identical. Nietzsche goes on to argue that even this
   law is not basic but developed gradually.

3 Quoted in Curt Paul Janz, *Friedrich Nietzsche: Biographie*, 3 vols
   (Munich, 1978), vol. I, p. 696.

4 It was reprinted with the addition of 'Vermischte Meinungen und
   Sprüche' (*VMS*, 1879); *The Wanderer and His Shadow* (*WS*) was published
   separately in 1880; both were incorporated in the new edition of
   Human, All-Too-Human, published in 1886.

5 Quoted in W. D. Williams, *Nietzsche and the French* (Oxford, 1952),
   p. 37. See also Brendan Donnellan, *Nietzsche and the French Moralists*
   (Bonn, 1982).

6 Williams, *Nietzsche and the French*, p. 126.

7 Sander L. Gilman, ed., *Conversations with Nietzsche: A Life in the Words of His Contemporaries* (New York, 1991), p. 113.

8 The fifth book of *The Gay Science*, 'We Fearless Ones', was added only in 1887.

9 On Nietzsche's admiration for Voltaire, see Thomas Brobjer, *Nietzsche's Philosophical Context: An Intellectual Biography* (Urbana, IL, 2008), p. 63. On his Enlightenment, see Henning Ottmann, *Philosophie und Politik bei Nietzsche* (Berlin, 1987), p. 175; Mazzino Montinari, 'Aufklärung und Revolution: Nietzsche und der späte Goethe', in *Nietzsche lesen* (Berlin, 1982), pp. 56–63; Nicholas Martin, '"Aufklärung und kein Ende": The Place of Enlightenment in Friedrich Nietzsche's Thought', *German Life and Letters*, LXI (2008), pp. 79–97.

10 Similarly, Nietzsche's Basel friend and colleague Overbeck, in his iconoclastic book *Über die Christlichkeit unserer heutigen Theologie* (repr. Darmstadt, 1963), described Christianity as a mummified version of ancient culture (p. 22).

11 See Lucretius, *On the Nature of the Universe*, trans. Ronald Latham (Harmondsworth, 1952), pp. 206–9; David Hume, *The Natural History of Religion*, ed. A. Wayne Colver (Oxford, 1976), p. 36.

12 Nietzsche learned about animism especially from the British anthropologist Sir John Lubbock. See *HA* 111; Lubbock, *The Origin of Civilisation and the Primitive Condition of Man: Mental and Social Condition of Savages* (London, 1870); and David S. Thatcher, 'Nietzsche's Debt to Lubbock', *Journal of the History of Ideas*, XLIV (1983), pp. 293–309.

13 'Le *moi* est haïssable': Blaise Pascal, *Pensées*, ed. Louis Lafuma (Paris, 1973), p. 76.

14 Nietzsche is not exaggerating here: see Jean Delumeau, *Le Péché et la peur: La culpabilisation en Occident, XIIIe–XVIIIe siècles* (Paris, 1983); Ritchie Robertson, *The Enlightenment: The Pursuit of Happiness, 1680–1790* (London, 2020), pp. 215–19.

15 This argument was put forward in 1739 by David Hume: see *A Treatise of Human Nature: A Critical Edition*, ed. David Fate Norton and Mary J. Norton (Oxford, 2007), p. 114 (Book I, section iii, para. 14). It aroused Kant from his 'dogmatic slumbers' and prompted him to reply in the *Critique of Pure Reason* (1781). Nietzsche probably knew Hume's work only indirectly, from Lange and other sources.

16 See the critical discussions in Maudemarie Clark, *Nietzsche on Truth and Philosophy* (Cambridge, 1990), pp. 63–77; Bernard Williams, *Truth and Truthfulness* (Princeton, NJ, 2002), pp. 21–8.

17 Clark, *Nietzsche on Truth and Philosophy*, p. 87.

18 Gregory Moore, *Nietzsche, Biology and Metaphor* (Cambridge, 2002), p. 37.

19 See ibid., p. 44.

20 See Hume, 'A Dialogue', in *An Enquiry concerning the Principles of Morals*, ed. Tom L. Beauchamp (Oxford, 1998).

21 Prosper Merimée, *Lettres à une inconnue*, 2 vols (Paris, 1874), vol. I, p. 8.

22 Cf. Hume: 'When the deity is represented as infinitely superior to mankind, this belief, tho' altogether just, is apt, when joined with superstitious terrors, to sink the human mind into the lowest submission and abasement, and to represent the monkish virtues of mortification, pennance [*sic*], humility, and passive suffering, as the only qualities which are acceptable to him' (*Natural History of Religion*, p. 62).

23 'I am but little given to pity, and I could wish I was not so at all. Though there is nothing I would not do to comfort an afflicted person, and I really believe that one should do all one can to show great sympathy to him for his misfortune, for miserable people are so foolish that this does them the greatest good in the world; yet I also hold that we should be content with expressing sympathy, and carefully avoid having any. It is a passion that is wholly worthless in a well-regulated mind, which only serves to weaken the heart, and which should be left to ordinary persons, who, as they never do anything from reason, have need of passions to stimulate their actions.' La Rochefoucauld, *Oeuvres complètes* (Paris, 1964), pp. 5–6. My translation.

24 Small's translation is entitled *History of the Moral Sensations*, but I prefer *Sentiments*, because it recalls the Enlightenment analyses of morality on which Rée was drawing, such as Adam Smith's *Theory of Moral Sentiments* (1759). Nietzsche later claimed, implausibly, to have disagreed with the book from the outset (*GM* preface 4).

25 Paul Rée, *The Origin of the Moral Sensations*, in his *Basic Writings*, ed. Robin Small (Urbana, IL, 2003), p. 98. Rée, like Nietzsche, follows Lubbock's account of primitive thought. Nietzsche will of course reject this argument later (*GM* I 2), but for now he accepts it (*GS* 39).

26 William James, 'The Dilemma of Determinism', in his *The Will to Believe and Other Essays in Popular Philosophy* (New York, 1956), pp. 145–83 (p. 149).

27 Some recent political theorists have tried to derive from Nietzsche a concept of 'agonistic democracy'. See Hugo Drochon, *Nietzsche's Great Politics* (Princeton, NJ, 2016), pp. 71–5, and Christa Davis Acampora, 'Agonistic Communities: Love, War and Spheres of Activity', in *Conflict and Contest in Nietzsche's Philosophy*, ed. Herman Siemens and James Pearson (London, 2019), pp. 122–44. It is unclear, however, how such democracy could be embodied in political institutions.

4 The Prophet

1 For her later literary career (as Lou Andreas-Salomé), her relationship with the poet Rainer Maria Rilke and her training in psychoanalysis with Freud, see Angela Livingstone, *Lou Andreas-Salomé: Her Life and Writings* (London, 1984).

2 Lou Andreas-Salomé, *Lebensrückblick*, ed. Ernst Pfeiffer (Frankfurt a.M., 1968), p. 80.

3 Sue Prideaux, *I Am Dynamite! A Life of Friedrich Nietzsche* (London, 2018), p. 206; Prideaux provides a detailed and evocative description of Monte Sacro, pp. 204–6.

4 *Thus Spoke Zarathustra*, trans. Graham Parkes (Oxford, 2005), p. 291.

5 Parkes, whose excellent translation I mostly follow, misleadingly translates 'die glückseligen Inseln' as 'the Isles of the Blest', implying a kind of paradise; they are, however, clearly an earthly location on a shipping route.

6 Laurence Lampert, *Nietzsche's Teaching: An Interpretation of 'Thus Spoke Zarathustra'* (New Haven, CT, 1986), p. 212. Cf. *EH* 'Wise' 3: 'the "eternal recurrence", my truly *abyss-deep* thought'.

7 Cf. Nietzsche's letter of 29 August 1883 to Elisabeth, quoted above.

8 Cf. *D* preface 3, where 'the moral tarantula Rousseau' is held responsible for the French Revolution.

9 For example Jacques Derrida, *Spurs: Nietzsche's Styles*, trans. Barbara Harlow (Chicago, IL, 1979); cf. Keith Ansell-Pearson, *An Introduction to Nietzsche as Political Thinker* (Cambridge, 1994), pp. 188–9.

10 On all these, see the biographical sketches in Carol Diethe, *Nietzsche's Women: Beyond the Whip* (Berlin, 1996), pp. 77–100.

11 Sander L. Gilman, ed., *Conversations with Nietzsche: A Life in the Words of His Contemporaries* (New York, 1991), pp. 124–5; Diethe, *Nietzsche's Women*, pp. 63–4.

12 See Robert C. Holub, *Nietzsche in the Nineteenth Century: Social Questions and Philosophical Interventions* (Philadelphia, PA, 2018), p. 213.

13 I have adopted Graham Parkes's translation 'Overhuman', though Nietzsche nowhere implies that the Overhuman could possibly be female.

14 See Gregory Moore, *Nietzsche, Biology and Metaphor* (Cambridge, 2002), p. 136.

15 Walter Kaufmann, *Nietzsche: Philosopher, Psychologist, Antichrist*, 4th edn (Princeton, NJ, 1974), p. 316.

16 Jacob Burckhardt, *The Civilization of the Renaissance*, trans. S.G.C. Middlemore (Oxford, 1944), p. 2.

17 Ibid., p. 72.

18 Karl Löwith, *Nietzsche's Philosophy of the Eternal Recurrence of the Same*, trans. J. Harvey Lomax (Berkeley, CA, 1997), p. 117. St Augustine reviews and rebuts these theories in *The City of God*, Book XIV, chs 12–14.

19 For the pre-Socratics, see Nietzsche, *Die Philosophie im tragischen Zeitalter der Griechen* (*KSA* I 829). For a famous expression of the Platonic conception, see the chorus in Shelley's lyrical drama *Hellas* (1822) beginning 'The world's great age begins anew' (*The Complete Poetical Works of Shelley*, ed. Thomas Hutchinson (London, 1934), p. 477).

20 Lou Andreas-Salomé, *Friedrich Nietzsche in seinen Werken*, ed. Ernst Pfeiffer (Frankfurt a.M., 1983; first published 1894), p. 255.

21 In a notebook entry, Nietzsche says that the eternal recurrence is 'the most scientific of all possible hypotheses', but also that it is 'the most extreme form of nihilism: nothingness (meaninglessness) for ever!' (*KSA* XII 213).

22 On Nietzsche's (mistaken) premises, this means not only that the present world will recur, but that all possible worlds will come into being and recur infinitely many times. There will be innumerable

worlds in which I am not born; worlds in which I exist, but in constant pain; worlds in which Napoleon conquers the globe; worlds in which the dinosaurs survive and humanity never emerges; and so on. Yet such wild speculations are tame besides those of modern physics about a multiverse constantly generating innumerable parallel universes.

23 Kaufmann, *Nietzsche*, p. 322.
24 Ibid., p. 320.
25 Maudemarie Clark, *Nietzsche on Truth and Philosophy* (Cambridge, 1990), p. 268; Bernard Reginster, *The Affirmation of Life: Nietzsche on Overcoming Nihilism* (Cambridge, MA, 2006), p. 211.
26 Curt Paul Janz, *Friedrich Nietzsche: Biographie*, 3 vols (Munich, 1978), vol. II, p. 280.
27 Andreas-Salomé, *Friedrich Nietzsche*, p. 253.
28 Lampert in Paul Bishop, ed., *A Companion to Friedrich Nietzsche: Life and Works* (Rochester, NY, 2012), pp. 204–5, 225–6.
29 William James, *The Varieties of Religious Experience* (London, 1903), p. 41.
30 See Christopher Janaway, *Beyond Selflessness: Reading Nietzsche's 'Genealogy'* (Oxford, 2007), p. 258.
31 See David Benatar, *Better Never to Have Been: The Harm of Coming into Existence* (Oxford, 2006).
32 Holub, *Nietzsche in the Nineteenth Century*, p. 404.
33 Moore, *Nietzsche, Biology and Metaphor*, pp. 37, 43.
34 Holub, *Nietzsche in the Nineteenth Century*, p. 405.
35 Clark, *Nietzsche on Truth and Philosophy*, p. 206; Peter Poellner, *Nietzsche and Metaphysics* (Oxford, 1995), p. 15.
36 Janz, *Friedrich Nietzsche*, vol. II, pp. 222–3.
37 See Peter Sprengel, *Geschichte der deutschsprachigen Literatur 1870–1900* (Munich, 1998), pp. 224–5.
38 See Raymond Furness, *Zarathustra's Children: A Study of a Lost Generation of German Writers* (Rochester, NY, 2000).
39 Steven E. Aschheim, *The Nietzsche Legacy in Germany, 1890–1990* (Berkeley, CA, 1992), pp. 34–5.
40 Ibid., p. 135.
41 J. P. Stern, *A Study of Nietzsche* (Cambridge, 1979), p. 158. For an array of further criticisms, see Furness, *Zarathustra's Children*, pp. 4–5.

5 The Philosopher with the Hammer

1 Sander L. Gilman, ed., *Conversations with Nietzsche: A Life in the Words of His Contemporaries* (New York, 1991), p. 183.
2 Ibid., p. 168.
3 Ibid., p. 195.
4 Ibid., p. 168.
5 Ibid., p. 163.
6 Ibid., p. 165.
7 See Thomas Brobjer, *Nietzsche's Philosophical Context: An Intellectual Biography* (Urbana, IL, 2008), pp. 90–104.
8 See Walther Rauschenberger, 'Aus der letzten Lebenszeit Philipp Mainländers. Nach ungedruckten Briefen und Aufzeichnungen des Philosophen', *Süddeutsche Monatshefte*, 9 (1911–12), pp. 117–31. Nietzsche mentions Mainländer (*GS* 357), wrongly thinking he was a Jew.
9 J. W. Burrow, *The Crisis of Reason: European Thought, 1848–1914* (New Haven, CT, 2000), p. 61.
10 Robin Small, *Nietzsche in Context* (Aldershot, 2001), p. 91.
11 Quoted in Curt Paul Janz, *Friedrich Nietzsche: Biographie*, 3 vols (Munich, 1978), vol. II, pp. 447–8.
12 Gilman, *Conversations*, p. 153.
13 Cf. *CW* 1 and the enthusiasm Nietzsche expressed to acquaintances (Gilman, *Conversations*, pp. 131, 150); but he told the composer Carl Fuchs that he had only praised Bizet to play him off against Wagner (27 December 1888), and though Bizet provided a welcome respite, it seems unlikely that he really thought Bizet Wagner's equal.
14 See Ben Macintyre, *Forgotten Fatherland: The Search for Elisabeth Nietzsche* (London, 1992).
15 Gilman, *Conversations*, p. 148.
16 For a vivid and sympathetic view of this phase of Nietzsche's life, see Lesley Chamberlain, *Nietzsche in Turin: The End of the Future* (London, 1996).
17 Janz, *Friedrich Nietzsche*, vol. III, p. 30. On the dating of Nietzsche's collapse, see ibid., p. 34.
18 Gilman, *Conversations*, pp. 237–8.

19 See Brian Leiter, 'The Paradox of Fatalism and Self-Creation in Nietzsche', in *Willing and Nothingness: Schopenhauer as Nietzsche's Educator*, ed. Christopher Janaway (Oxford, 1998), pp. 217–57.

20 Georg Christoph Lichtenberg, *Schriften und Briefe*, ed. Wolfgang Promies, 4 vols (Munich, 1967–72), vol. II, p. 412.

21 Hume similarly, in 1739, defines the self as 'nothing but a bundle or collection of different impressions, which succeed each other with an inconceivable rapidity, and are in a perpetual flux and movement' (*Treatise*, p. 165 (Book I, section 4, para. 6)). For a comparison with Nietzsche, see Peter E. J. Kail, 'Hume and Nietzsche', in *The Oxford Handbook of Hume*, ed. Paul Russell (Oxford, 2016), pp. 755–79. According to Julian Baggini, Hume's view is now the most popular one among academic philosophers, psychologists and neuroscientists, and is supported by our knowledge of brain circuitry, while the great philosophies of Asia likewise maintain that the individual self is illusory: Baggini, *How the World Thinks: A Global History of Philosophy* (London, 2018), pp. 186–7, 175–84.

22 Cf. William Blake, 'One Law for the Lion and Ox Is Oppression', in *Complete Writings*, ed. Geoffrey Keynes (London, 1972), p. 158.

23 Christopher Janaway, *Beyond Selflessness: Reading Nietzsche's 'Genealogy'* (Oxford, 2007), p. 114.

24 Cf. *TI* 'Excursions' 49, where Nietzsche praises Goethe for his 'joyful and trusting fatalism' (see, for example, the ending of Goethe's poem 'Seefahrt').

25 Cf.: 'a man strong in character considers this most of all, that all things follow from the necessity of the divine nature'; Benedict de Spinoza, *Ethics*, trans. Edwin Curley (London, 1996), p. 154 (Book IV, p. 73).

26 This sentence also occurs in *Zarathustra* IV 9, spoken by Zarathustra's Shadow, who finds this insight painful and has not yet learned to rejoice at it.

27 Derrida, quoted in Maudemarie Clark, *Nietzsche on Truth and Philosophy* (Cambridge, 1990), p. 18.

28 Nietzsche took this idea from a work by his one-time Basel colleague Gustav Teichmüller, *Die wirkliche und die scheinbare Welt* (1882), which maintains that all knowledge, other than that of the self, is merely a semiotic or sign-language; even our knowledge of our own feelings and thoughts is constructed semiotically, that is, is an interpretation (see

Small, *Nietzsche in Context*, p. 44). Teichmüller wrote: 'The world, as it appears to the eye, is always and everywhere ordered into perspectives, and neither microscope nor telescope can show us the order of things which we hold to be the real one. [. . .] It requires that one recognizes the *cause* of the perspectival appearance' (quoted in Brobjer, *Nietzsche's Philosophical Context*, p. 97). Nietzsche goes beyond Teichmüller in denying even the existence of a stable self.

29 For example Richard Schacht, *Nietzsche* (London, 1983), pp. 8–10.

30 Alexander Nehamas, *Nietzsche: Life as Literature* (Cambridge, MA, 1985), p. 66.

31 To develop Nietzsche's metaphor of seeing: as we have two eyes, we already have two perspectives, each of which corrects the other. Further: if I want to find out about anything, I have to collect a number of perspectives – for example if I want to write about recent British politics, I will consult spokesmen of all political parties, Brexiteers and Remainers, a range of political commentators and an equally wide range of members of the public. My account will then be formed by all these perspectives. See E. D. Hirsch, 'Faulty Perspectives', in *The Aims of Interpretation* (Chicago, IL, 1976), pp. 36–49.

32 Clark, *Nietzsche on Truth and Philosophy*, p. 143.

33 For example Walter Charleton's *Natural History of the Passions* (1674); La Mettrie's *Histoire naturelle de l'âme* (1746); Hume's *Natural History of Religion* (1757); W.E.H. Lecky, 'The Natural History of Morals', ch. 1 of his *History of European Morals* (1869).

34 See Christian J. Emden, *Friedrich Nietzsche and the Politics of History* (Cambridge, 2008).

35 Seneca, 'De clementia/On mercy', *Moral Essays*, trans. John W. Basore, 3 vols (Cambridge, MA, 1970), vol. I, pp. 441, 443. See Martha C. Nussbaum, 'Pity and Mercy: Nietzsche's Stoicism', in *Nietzsche, Genealogy, Morality: Essays on Nietzsche's 'On the Genealogy of Morals'*, ed. Richard Schacht (Berkeley, CA, 1994), pp. 139–67. Cf. Nietzsche on La Rochefoucauld, ch. 3 above.

36 *Grundlegung der Metaphysik der Sitten*, in Immanuel Kant, *Werke*, ed. Wilhelm Weischedel, 6 vols (Darmstadt, 1956–64), vol. IV, p. 24.

37 For example Raymond Geuss, 'Nietzsche and Genealogy', in *Morality, Culture, and History: Essays on German Philosophy* (Cambridge, 1999), pp. 1–28; Emden, *Friedrich Nietzsche and the*

Politics of History, pp. 230–32. Such commentators are often influenced by Michel Foucault's essay 'Nietzsche, la généalogie, l'histoire' (1971); see 'Nietzsche, Genealogy, History', in *The Foucault Reader*, ed. Paul Rabinow (Harmondsworth, 1986), pp. 76–100, and for criticism, Robert C. Holub, 'Reading Nietzsche as Postmodernist: Rhetoric, Genealogy, Perspectivism in Ahistorical Context', in *Why Literature Matters: Theories and Functions of Literature*, ed. Rüdiger Ahrens and Laurenz Volkmann (Heidelberg, 1996), pp. 247–63.

38 Cf. the passage in the 1885–6 notebooks where Nietzsche lists the 'usual errors of historians of morality' (*Moral-Historiker*), *KSA* XII 145.

39 For a list of Nietzsche's reading in this area, see Anthony K. Jensen, *Nietzsche's Philosophy of History* (Cambridge, 2013), p. 159n. A full study remains to be undertaken.

40 Janaway, *Beyond Selflessness*, p. 12.

41 Similarly in letter to Köselitz, 31 May 1888.

42 See Burrow, *The Crisis of Reason*, pp. 106–7; A. L. Basham, *The Wonder that Was India*, 3rd edn (London, 1967), pp. 29–32.

43 Recent commentators on *The Genealogy of Morals* (for example Janaway, *Beyond Selflessness*) have understandably steered clear of this passage, which disturbingly recalls the racial fantasies of Arthur de Gobineau (1816–1882) and their later influence on Nazi ideology. However, Nietzsche knew little of Gobineau; he is only incidentally concerned with 'race', far more with morality and culture; and his idiosyncratic speculations on the racial future of Europe (see below) were quite different from Gobineau's lament for the decline of the white race: see Nicholas Martin, 'Breeding Greeks: Nietzsche, Gobineau, and Classical Theories of Race', in *Nietzsche and Antiquity*, ed. Paul Bishop (Rochester, NY, 2004), pp. 40–53; Hugo Drochon, *Nietzsche's Great Politics* (Princeton, NJ, 2016), p. 85. He uses the word *Rasse* (race) only loosely: 'the Latin races' (*BGE* 48); 'the hard-working races' (*BGE* 189). He sharply distinguishes his own ideas about race from 'crude chatter about "Aryan"' (*KSA* XI 50).

44 See Drochon, *Nietzsche's Great Politics*, pp. 55–6. Cf. Hume, 'Of the Original Contract' [1747]: 'Almost all the governments which exist at present, or of which there remains any record in story, have been founded originally either on usurpation or conquest, or both, without any pretence of a fair consent or voluntary subjection of the people' (*Essays* (Oxford, 1963), p. 457).

45 Although some of Nietzsche's best expositors claim that the 'blond beast' *only* denotes a lion (Walter Kaufmann, *Nietzsche: Philosopher, Psychologist, Antichrist*, 4th edn (Princeton, NJ, 1974), p. 225; Martin, 'Breeding Greeks', p. 47), the image strongly suggests contemporary ideas about fair-haired Aryans, though Nietzsche extends it to predatory types from other races (Arabs, Japanese): see Gregory Moore, *Nietzsche, Biology and Metaphor* (Cambridge, 2002), p. 157; Drochon, *Nietzsche's Great Politics*, p. 84.

46 Nietzsche found *Ressentiment* used in Eugen Dühring's *Der Werth des Lebens* (1865), on which he made extensive notes in 1875: see *KSA* VIII 131–81 (p. 176); Aldo Venturelli, 'Asketismus und Wille zur Macht. Nietzsches Auseinandersetzung mit Eugen Dühring', *Nietzsche-Studien*, 15 (1986), pp. 107–39 (pp. 131–2).

47 Nietzsche took the passage from the rationalist historian Lecky: see W.E.H. Lecky, *The Rise and Influence of Rationalism in Europe*, 2 vols, new edn (London, 1897), vol. I, pp. 324–5; cf. Jean Delumeau, *Le Péché et la peur: La culpabilisation en Occident, XIIIᵉ–XVIIIᵉ siècles* (Paris, 1983), pp. 457–8.

48 See Richard J. Evans, *Rituals of Retribution: Capital Punishment in Germany, 1600–1987* (Oxford, 1996), pp. 35–41.

49 Stendhal says this in the travel book *Rome, Naples et Florence* (1854) (note in Douglas Smith's translation of *GM*, p. 152).

50 Cf. the attack on vegetarianism in letter to Carl von Gersdorff, 28 September 1869.

51 Janaway, *Beyond Selflessness*, p. 211.

52 Nietzsche's project thus has something in common with such classics of cultural history as his friend Jacob Burckhardt's *The Civilization of the Renaissance in Italy* (1860) and Johan Huizinga's *The Autumn of the Middle Ages* (1919).

53 Opening of 'On Truth and Lie', *KSA* I 875.

54 Nietzsche is here reversing contemporary psychological theories which saw the criminal as degenerate: see Moore, *Nietzsche, Biology and Metaphor*, p. 171.

55 Nietzsche is continuing the Enlightenment attack on 'priestcraft', that is, the falsification and exploitation of religion by power-hungry priests. See Ritchie Robertson, *The Enlightenment: The Pursuit of Happiness, 1680–1790* (London, 2020), p. 222. On his debt to Wellhausen,

who argued that priestly Judaism moved ever further from nature, see Andreas Urs Sommer, *Friedrich Nietzsches 'Der Antichrist': Ein philosophisch-historischer Kommentar* (Basel, 2000), p. 244.

56 Cf. Ernest Renan, *Vie de Jésus* (Paris, 1870): 'Dieu est en lui; il se sent avec Dieu' (p. 40). Nietzsche, perhaps to conceal his own debt, seriously misrepresents Renan's book (*A* 29).

57 Cf. Dostoevsky's description of the ecstasy preceding an epileptic fit, *The Idiot*, trans. Constance Garnett (London, 1946), pp. 219–20.

58 Occurrences of this phrase in the late books are helpfully listed in Janaway, *Beyond Selflessness*, p. 13n.

59 Compare *A* 57 with KSA XIII 386.

60 Drochon, *Nietzsche's Great Politics*, p. 99.

61 See Robert C. Holub, *Nietzsche in the Nineteenth Century: Social Questions and Philosophical Interventions* (Philadelphia, PA, 2018), pp. 427–53; Holub also surveys the many reflections in Nietzsche's late notebooks on how marriage and procreation might be regulated.

62 See Diane Paul, 'Eugenics and the Left', *Journal of the History of Ideas*, XLV (1984), pp. 567–90.

63 Dan Stone, *Breeding Superman: Nietzsche, Race and Eugenics in Edwardian and Interwar Britain* (Liverpool, 2002).

64 John Richardson, *Nietzsche's New Darwinism* (Oxford, 2004), p. 192.

65 The neutral-sounding 'variants' softens Nietzsche's original term, *die Abartenden*, meaning those who degenerate from the aristocracy's standards.

66 Steven E. Aschheim, *The Nietzsche Legacy in Germany, 1890–1990* (Berkeley, CA, 1992), pp. 232–52; Max Whyte, 'The Uses and Abuses of Nietzsche in the Third Reich: Alfred Baeumler's "Heroic Realism"', *Journal of Contemporary History*, XLII (2008), pp. 171–94. The collection of essays edited by Jacob Golomb and Robert S. Wistrich, *Nietzsche: Godfather of Fascism?* (Princeton, NJ, 2002), is lacking in historical studies (as a contributor notes, p. 123).

67 Bertrand Russell, 'The Free Man's Worship', in *Philosophical Essays* (London, 1910), pp. 60–61.

68 'Large Red Man Reading', in Wallace Stevens, *Collected Poems* (London, 1955), p. 423.

69 See Blake, 'The Marriage of Heaven and Hell', Plate 4, in *Complete Writings*, p. 149; on Goethe, see especially the speech by the Earth

Spirit: 'Birth and the grave,/ An eternal wave,/ Turning, returning,/ A life ever burning' (Goethe, *Faust Part One*, trans. David Luke (Oxford, 1987), p. 19).

70 Robertson, *The Enlightenment*, pp. 261–350; Steven Pinker, *The Better Angels of Our Nature: The Decline of Violence in History and Its Causes* (London, 2011).

Bibliography

(Confined to works in English)

Abbey, Ruth, *Nietzsche's Middle Period* (Oxford, 2000)
Allison, David R., ed., *The New Nietzsche: Contemporary Styles of Interpretation* (Cambridge, MA, 1985)
Ansell-Pearson, Keith, *An Introduction to Nietzsche as Political Thinker* (Cambridge, 1994)
—, ed., *Nietzsche and Modern German Thought* (London, 2002)
Aschheim, Steven E., *The Nietzsche Legacy in Germany, 1890–1990* (Berkeley, CA, 1992)
Bergmann, Peter, *Nietzsche: 'The Last Antipolitical German'* (Bloomington, IN, 1987)
Berkowitz, Peter, *Nietzsche: The Ethics of an Immoralist* (Cambridge, MA, 1995)
Bishop, Paul, *The Dionysian Self: C. G. Jung's Reception of Friedrich Nietzsche* (Berlin, 1995)
—, ed., *A Companion to Friedrich Nietzsche: Life and Works* (Rochester, NY, 2012)
—, ed., *Nietzsche and Antiquity: His Reaction and Response to the Classical Tradition* (Rochester, NY, 2004)
Borchmeyer, Dieter, 'Wagner and Nietzsche', in *Wagner Handbook*, ed. Ulrich Müller and Peter Wapnewski (Cambridge, MA, 1992), pp. 327–42
Bridgwater, Patrick, *Nietzsche in Anglosaxony* (Leicester, 1972)
Brobjer, Thomas, *Nietzsche's Philosophical Context: An Intellectual Biography* (Urbana, IL, 2008)
Brunkhorst, Katja, *'Verwandt-Verwandelt': Nietzsche's Presence in Rilke* (Munich, 2006)
Cate, Curtis, *Friedrich Nietzsche* (London, 2002)

Chamberlain, Lesley, *Nietzsche in Turin: The End of the Future* (London, 1996)

Clark, Maudemarie, *Nietzsche on Truth and Philosophy* (Cambridge, 1990)

Derrida, Jacques, *Spurs: Nietzsche's Styles*, trans. Barbara Harlow (Chicago, IL, 1979)

Detwiler, Bruce, *Nietzsche and the Politics of Aristocratic Radicalism* (Chicago, IL, 1990)

Diethe, Carol, *Nietzsche's Women: Beyond the Whip* (Berlin, 1996)

Donnellan, Brendan, *Nietzsche and the French Moralists* (Bonn, 1982)

Dries, Manuel, ed., *Nietzsche on Time and History* (Berlin, 2008)

Drochon, Hugo, *Nietzsche's Great Politics* (Princeton, NJ, 2016)

Emden, Christian J., *Friedrich Nietzsche and the Politics of History* (Cambridge, 2008)

—, *Nietzsche on Language, Consciousness and the Body* (Urbana, IL, 2005)

—, *Nietzsche's Naturalism: Philosophy and the Life Sciences in the Nineteenth Century* (Cambridge, 2014)

Foucault, Michel, 'Nietzsche, Genealogy, History', in *The Foucault Reader*, ed. Paul Rabinow (Harmondsworth, 1986), pp. 76–100

Furness, Raymond, *Zarathustra's Children: A Study of a Lost Generation of German Writers* (Rochester, NY, 2000)

Gemes, Ken, and John Richardson, eds, *The Oxford Handbook of Nietzsche* (Oxford, 2013)

Geuss, Raymond, 'Nietzsche and Genealogy', in *Morality, Culture, and History: Essays on German Philosophy* (Cambridge, 1999), pp. 1–28

Gilman, Sander L., ed., *Conversations with Nietzsche: A Life in the Words of His Contemporaries* (New York, 1991)

—, Carole Blair and David J. Parent, ed. and trans., *Friedrich Nietzsche on Rhetoric and Language* (New York, 1989)

Golomb, Jacob, ed., *Nietzsche and Jewish Culture* (London, 1997)

—, and Robert S. Wistrich, eds, *Nietzsche: Godfather of Fascism?* (Princeton, NJ, 2002)

Hayman, Ronald, *Nietzsche: A Critical Life* (London, 1980)

Hollinrake, Roger, *Nietzsche, Wagner and the Philosophy of Pessimism* (London, 1982)

Holub, Robert C., 'Reading Nietzsche as Postmodernist: Rhetoric, Genealogy, Perspectivism in Ahistorical Context', in *Why Literature Matters: Theories and Functions of Literature*, ed. Rüdiger Ahrens and Laurenz Volkmann (Heidelberg, 1996), pp. 247–63

—, *Nietzsche in the Nineteenth Century: Social Questions and Philosophical Interventions* (Philadelphia, PA, 2018)

Janaway, Christopher, *Beyond Selflessness: Reading Nietzsche's 'Genealogy'* (Oxford, 2007)

—, ed., *Willing and Nothingness: Schopenhauer as Nietzsche's Educator* (Oxford, 1998)

Jensen, Anthony K., *Nietzsche's Philosophy of History* (Cambridge, 2013)

Kail, Peter E. J., 'Hume and Nietzsche', in *The Oxford Handbook of Hume*, ed. Paul Russell (Oxford, 2016), pp. 755–79

Kaufmann, Walter, *Nietzsche: Philosopher, Psychologist, Antichrist*, 4th edn (Princeton, NJ, 1974)

Lampert, Laurence, *Nietzsche's Task: An Interpretation of 'Beyond Good and Evil'* (New Haven, CT, 2001)

—, *Nietzsche's Teaching: An Interpretation of 'Thus Spoke Zarathustra'* (New Haven, CT, 1986)

Leiter, Brian, *Nietzsche and Morality* (Oxford, 2007)

Löwith, Karl, *Nietzsche's Philosophy of the Eternal Recurrence of the Same*, trans. J. Harvey Lomax (Berkeley, CA, 1997)

Macintyre, Ben, *Forgotten Fatherland: The Search for Elisabeth Nietzsche* (London, 1992)

Martin, Nicholas, '"Aufklärung und kein Ende": The Place of Enlightenment in Friedrich Nietzsche's Thought', *German Life and Letters*, 61 (2008), pp. 79–97

—, 'Fighting a Philosophy: The Figure of Nietzsche in British Propaganda of the First World War', *Modern Language Review*, 98 (2003), pp. 367–80

—, ed., *Nietzsche and the German Tradition* (Bern, 2003)

May, Keith M., *Nietzsche and Modern Literature: Themes in Yeats, Rilke, Mann and Lawrence* (Basingstoke, 1988)

May, Simon, *Nietzsche's Ethics and His War on 'Morality'* (Cambridge, 1999)

—, ed., *Nietzsche's 'On the Genealogy of Morality': A Critical Guide* (Cambridge, 2011)

Montinari, Mazzino, *Reading Nietzsche*, trans. Greg Whittock (Urbana, IL, 2003)

Moore, Gregory, *Nietzsche, Biology and Metaphor* (Cambridge, 2002)

Nehamas, Alexander, *Nietzsche: Life as Literature* (Cambridge, MA, 1985)

Nicholls, R. A., *Nietzsche in the Early Works of Thomas Mann* (Berkeley, CA, 1955)

O'Flaherty, James C., Timothy F. Sellner and Robert M. Helm, eds, *Studies in Nietzsche and the Classical Tradition* (Chapel Hill, NC, 1976)

—, eds, *Studies in Nietzsche and the Judaeo-Christian Tradition* (Chapel Hill, NC, 1985)

Parkes, Graham, ed., *Nietzsche and Asian Thought* (Chicago, IL, 1991)

Pasley, Malcolm, ed., *Nietzsche: Imagery and Thought* (London, 1978)

Poellner, Peter, *Nietzsche and Metaphysics* (Oxford, 1995)

Prideaux, Sue, *I Am Dynamite! A Life of Friedrich Nietzsche* (London, 2018)

Reginster, Bernard, *The Affirmation of Life: Nietzsche on Overcoming Nihilism* (Cambridge, MA, 2006)

Richardson, John, *Nietzsche's New Darwinism* (Oxford, 2004)

Ruehl, Martin A., 'Ruthless Renaissance: Burckhardt, Nietzsche, and the Violent Birth of the Modern Self ', in *The Italian Renaissance in the German Historical Imagination* (Cambridge, 2015), pp. 58–104

Schacht, Richard, *Nietzsche* (London, 1983)

—, ed., *Nietzsche, Genealogy, Morality: Essays on Nietzsche's 'On the Genealogy of Morals'* (Berkeley, CA, 1994)

Sedgwick, Peter R., ed., *Nietzsche: A Critical Reader* (Oxford, 1995)

Siemens, Herman, and James Pearson, eds, *Conflict and Contest in Nietzsche's Philosophy* (London, 2019)

Silk, M. S., and J. P. Stern, *Nietzsche on Tragedy* (Cambridge, 1981)

Small, Robin, *Nietzsche in Context* (Aldershot, 2001)

—, *Nietzsche and Rée: A Star Friendship* (Oxford, 2005)

Smith, Douglas, *Transvaluations: Nietzsche in France, 1872–1972* (Oxford, 1996)

Sokel, Walter H., 'Nietzsche and Kafka: The Dionysian Connection', in *Kafka for the Twenty-First Century*, ed. Stanley Corngold and Ruth V. Gross (Rochester, NY, 2011), pp. 64–74

Stack, George J., *Lange and Nietzsche* (Berlin, 1983)

—, *Nietzsche and Emerson: An Elective Affinity* (Athens, OH, 1992)

Stern, J. P., *A Study of Nietzsche* (Cambridge, 1979)

Stern, Tom, ed., *The New Cambridge Companion to Nietzsche* (Cambridge, 2019)

Stone, Dan, *Breeding Superman: Nietzsche, Race and Eugenics in Edwardian and Interwar Britain* (Liverpool, 2002)

Tanner, Michael, *Nietzsche: A Very Short Introduction* (Oxford, 2000)

Thatcher, David S., 'Nietzsche's Debt to Lubbock', *Journal of the History of Ideas*, XLIV (1983), pp. 293–309

—, *Nietzsche in England, 1890–1914: The Growth of a Reputation* (Toronto, 1970)

Williams, W. D., *Nietzsche and the French* (Oxford, 1952)

Wolin, Richard, *The Seduction of Unreason: The Intellectual Romance with Fascism from Nietzsche to Postmodernism* (Princeton, NJ, 2004)

Ziolkowski, Theodore, 'Zarathustra's Reincarnations: Literary Responses to Nietzsche's Work', *Modern Language Review*, CVII (2012), pp. 211–29

Acknowledgements

I am grateful to Marton Dornbach, Jennifer Gosett-Ferencei and Nicholas Martin for reading and commenting on the entire manuscript.

Photo Acknowledgements

The author and publishers wish to express their thanks to the below sources of illustrative material and/or permission to reproduce it. Some locations of artworks are also given below, in the interest of brevity:

Agencja Fotograficzna Caro/Alamy Stock Photo: p. 132; from Carl Albrecht Bernoulli, *Franz Overbeck und Friedrich Nietzsche: Eine Freundschaft*, vol. I (Jena, 1908), photo Robarts Library, University of Toronto: p. 48; ETH-Bibliothek Zürich, Bildarchiv: pp. 44, 46; Library of Congress, Prints and Photographs Division, Washington, DC: p. 156; Museen Luzern: p. 88; Photothek des Zentralinstituts für Kunstgeschichte, Munich: p. 19; Süddeutsche Zeitung Photo/Alamy Stock Photo: p. 154; Thielska Galleriet, Stockholm (photos Tord Lund): pp. 159, 160; photo Torsade de Pointes: p. 115; Tufts University Digital Library, Medford, MA: p. 70.